The **N**

WORLD
POPULATION

'Publishers have created lists of short books that discuss the questions that your average [electoral] candidate will only ever touch if armed with a slogan and a soundbite. Together [such books] hint at a resurgence of the grand educational tradition... Closest to the hot headline issues are *The No-Nonsense Guides*. These target those topics that a large army of voters care about, but that politicos evade. Arguments, figures and documents combine to prove that good journalism is far too important to be left to (most) journalists.'

Boyd Tonkin,
The Independent,
London

About the author
Vanessa Baird is a co-editor of the *New Internationalist* magazine. Her previous books include The No-Nonsense Guide to Sexual Diversity (New Internationalist); Sex, Love and Homophobia (Amnesty International) and, as co-editor, People First Economics (New Internationalist).

Acknowledgements
Special thanks are due to Mohan Rao and Sarah Sexton for their detailed and insightful comments and suggestions. Any mistakes that remain are mine alone. Thanks are also due to several other writers and academics for their ground-breaking work – people like Betsy Hartmann, Matthew Connelly, Fred Pearce and David Satterthwaite who kindly wrote the Foreword.
  And finally, thanks to the book's editor Chris Brazier and its designer Andrew Kokotka, whose skill and professionalism are a pleasure.

Dedication
In memory of Jane Brodie, a kind and true friend who remained intelligently curious, passionately engaged and open-minded to the end. The last of our many long, deep and wide-ranging conversations set me on the journey that resulted in this book.

The  to

WORLD
POPULATION

Vanessa Baird

New Internationalist

BTL

The No-Nonsense Guide to World Population
Published in Canada by
New Internationalist™ Publications Ltd.   and Between the Lines
2446 Bank Street, Suite 653   401 Richmond Street West,
Ottawa, Ontario   Studio 277
K1V 1A8   Toronto, Ontario
www.newint.org   M5V 3A8
                                                 www.btlbooks.com

First published in the UK by
New Internationalist™ Publications Ltd
55 Rectory Road
Oxford OX4 1BW
New Internationalist is a registered trade mark.

Series editor: Chris Brazier
Design by New Internationalist Publications Ltd

Printed in UK by Bell and Bain Ltd.
who hold environmental accreditation ISO 14001.

Mixed Sources
Product group from well-managed
forests and other controlled sources
www.fsc.org   Cert no. TT-COC-002769
© 1996 Forest Stewardship Council

Library and Archives Canada Cataloguing in Publication

Baird, Vanessa
The no-nonsense guide to world population / Vanessa Baird

(No-nonsense guides)
Co-published by New Internationalist.
Includes index.
ISBN 978-1-926662-50-3

1. Population. 2. Population–Environmental aspects.
I. Title. II. Series: No-nonsense guides (Toronto, Ont.)
HB871.B34 2011   304.6   C2011-901532-3

Between the Lines gratefully acknowledges assistance for its publishing
activities from the Canada Council for the Arts, the Ontario Arts Council, the
Government of Ontario through the Ontario Book Publishers Tax Credit program
and through the Ontario Book Initiative, and the Government of Canada through
the Canada Book Fund.

  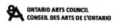

Canada   Canada Council   Conseil des Arts   ONTARIO ARTS COUNCIL
          for the Arts   du Canada   CONSEIL DES ARTS DE L'ONTARIO

Foreword

'There are shortages that threaten the world and the survival of humans and other species within it – scarcities of equity, justice, genuine democracy and respect for nature.'

'The "problem" with global population – if there is one – is too many rich people consuming too much, not too many poor people.'

'The idea that population pressure inevitably leads to increased land degradation is a much-repeated myth. It does not.'

These quotes from this book give a good sense of what it is about. 'Population is so often about something else, something other than sheer human numbers.' As this book describes, many of those lobbying for 'population control' are a pretty unsavory bunch. They use inaccurate or misleading statements about what they term 'over-population' as a cover for their racist views or their support for eugenics. They include the anti-immigration lobby in high-income nations who often exaggerate the scale of immigration. As this book points out, the countries with the biggest increase in refugees in recent years are actually not those with high incomes but those in Asia and Africa that are next to conflict-torn nations.

But as support for 'over-population' was waning in the 1990s, so the dangers posed by climate change came to be recognized and allowed a new set of inaccurate claims – this time regarding the contribution of population growth to climate change. If the impact of climate change is portrayed as tens of millions of immigrants rushing to high-income nations, it helps underpin completely inappropriate responses. If population growth is a major contributor to the growth in greenhouse-gas emissions, this will also underpin completely inappropriate responses. And neither of these responses do anything to address the underlying drivers of climate change – the high-consumption lifestyles of the wealthy and the fossil-fuel powered production system that caters for and encourages their demands.

'People are not pollution. Blaming too many people for driving climate change is like blaming too many trees for causing bush fires' (quoting Simon Butler).

But this book does recognize the need for more attention to supporting what might be called a population policy but is better termed the provision of healthcare services that include a strong focus on sexual and reproductive health. 'When women can make their own fertility choices, without pressure, without coercion, it is better for them, better for their families, better for their communities and better for the world too.'

When the needed equity, justice and genuine democracy mentioned above also means attention to the other needs of low-income groups – for secure housing, adequate livelihoods and access to water and sanitation – we know that this would bring dramatic reductions in infant, child and maternal mortality, and in population growth rates. But this too does not reduce the high-consumption lifestyles of the wealthy.

This is a very readable, jargon-free book that challenges the many myths and inaccuracies about population. In so doing, it also challenges us all to rethink what the real drivers of resource shortages, land degradation and global warming actually are.

David Satterthwaite
International Institute for Environment and Development (IIED)

CONTENTS

Introduction

WHEN SHE WAS young, my great-aunt – a tiny, sprightly woman who painted vast canvasses – had wanted to become a nun. Then she met a Flemish poet and they fell in love. She agreed to marry him on one condition: that they had 12 children. True to the old baking tradition, they made 13.

Her niece, my mother, also briefly flirted with the holy life. Her tryst with celibacy was equally convincing. As the eighth of her brood, I approach the subject of global population with a touch of trepidation. By most people's standard of reasonable family size I really shouldn't be here.

But then the subject of population – and in particular population growth – is one that seems capable of provoking all kinds of emotions.

Today there are around 7 billion people occupying this planet. That's up from 5.9 a decade ago. By 2050 it is projected to top 9 billion (see chart).

Talk of 'overpopulation' has been with us for some time. Already, in 1798, when there were a mere 978 million people in the world, mathematician Thomas Robert Malthus was warning of an impending catastrophe as human numbers exceeded the capacity to grow food.

He was, as it turned out, wrong. Population increased but so did farming efficiency.

Since then, the global history of counting people has gone through some murky periods, the most extreme human rights abuses having taken place under the mantle of 'population control'.

Often the real cause of concern was the fact that others – be they people of other races or social classes or religions or political allegiances – were reproducing themselves perhaps at a faster rate.

That attitude is not consigned to history. In 2009 Michael Laws, Mayor of Wanganui District in New

Zealand/Aotearoa, was proposing that in order to tackle the problems of child abuse and murder, members of the 'appalling underclass' should be paid not to have children. 'If we gave $10,000 to certain people and said "we'll voluntarily sterilize you" then all of society would be better off,' he told the *Dominion Post* newspaper.

Most contemporary worries about population are less offensively expressed. For many people the issue is primarily an environmental one. The logic is simple. The more people there are, the more greenhouse gas is emitted, the more damage is done. Any attempts to reduce carbon emissions will be negated by runaway population growth.

Food is another worry. Will there be enough to feed the world? Already one billion of us go hungry – what will it be like when another two or three billion join the planet? Many people are saying it will be a hell. The world is at breaking point; overpopulation will tip us over the edge.

Some are even saying we need fewer people than we currently have. The UK-based Optimum Population

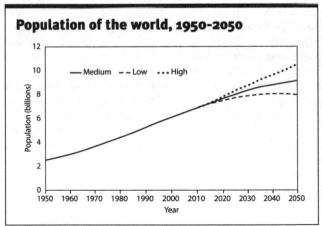

Population of the world, 1950-2050

Source: Population Division of the Department of Economic and Social Affairs of the United Nations Secretariat (2009). World Population Prospects: *The 2008 Revision*. New York: United Nations.

Trust is suggesting that to achieve sustainability we should be aiming to reduce global population by at least 1.7 billion people. The Voluntary Human Extinction Movement goes even further, saying that the best thing anyone can do for the Earth is to stop breeding altogether and give other species a chance at least of surviving the mess we have made.

On the other side are people who point out that such apocalyptic scenarios are not new; that, time and again, fears about population have concealed underlying problems of inequality and have been used to push other agendas, such as anti-immigration. Population is growing, they say, but we humans will do what we have always done faced with challenges: innovate, adapt, get more efficient, and use our ingenuity to survive.

Who is right? Should we be taking more notice of the ever louder clamor of alarm bells? Or is today's population panic as unfounded and potentially manipulative as earlier panics turned out to be? And is 'how many' people the main issue anyway?

Recently, I set out to do a special report on the subject for *New Internationalist* magazine. Back in the 1980s I'd been involved in producing press kits for the UN Population Fund. But that was a while ago. Since then I'd had only occasional contact with the issue and I didn't really know what to make of today's increasingly heated debates.

This book is a journey through what has become a veritable minefield. As the story of global population began to unfold I saw it to be a gripping narrative of life, death, sex, power, religion, money, food and the future of the planet itself.

The story begins with babies... or perhaps a little before that.

Vanessa Baird
Oxford, 2011

1 Are too many people being born?

Journalists and campaigners are sounding the alarm about population growth. But demographers don't seem to be panicking. Let's look at what they are studying: the numbers. And, in particular, at the birth rate.

SOMEONE HAS TAKEN the trouble to calculate that during the course of one day at least 200 million people on our planet will have sex.

Don't ask how they know or what definition of 'having sex' they are using. Suffice to say that it's happening and while, today, most of those people having sex will be using some form of contraception, many millions will not. Which might well contribute to the next figure.

Every 10 seconds – about the time it's taken you to read thus far – 44 people are born. That's around 140 million new babies over the course of a year. If you subtract the number of people who will die during the year, it's still adding another 83 million people to the world. That's the equivalent of another Germany or a quarter of the US.[1]

It mounts up, and in the gap between my writing this and your reading it, any precise figure for current global population will have become out of date. So let's settle for a nice round seven billion of us.

That's up from 5.9 billion a decade ago and by 2045-50 there are likely to be at least nine billion according to the UN's medium projection. Or there could be just under eight, if you go with the lowest projection. Or over 11 if you go with the highest.

Bewildered? You are not alone. But the middle projection of nine billion is the one that most demographers are going with, so let's stick with that (see chart page 13).

Before the 20th century no-one had ever witnessed

the doubling of global population. Now some people have lived through a tripling of it. And not so long ago, global population was a subject that fascinated few people apart from family planning professionals and demographers – a group of people described as being 'like accountants but without the charisma'.

Today, the dramatic escalation of human numbers is sprouting headlines across the world and causing agitated debate on the airwaves, in cyberspace and across kitchen tables. Such-and-such-a-number is 'too many people', someone confidently asserts. 'No, it isn't,' someone else counters, with equal confidence.

A trawl of headlines from various countries throws up the following:

'Global population explosion could cause wars and starvation' (*Daily Mirror*, Britain);

'How are we going to cope with the world's burgeoning population?'(*Brisbane Times*, Australia);

'Ageing populations may crimp the world's finances' (*New York Times*, US);

'Number of Muslims in Canada predicted to triple over next 20 years'(*National Post*, Canada);

'High population growth will be our doom' (*Daily Nation*, Kenya);

'Population time-bomb will hit Earth by 2020' (*Metro*, Britain);

'Population growth, climate change, grim pair' (*Victoria Times Colonist*, Canada);

'Population tide may turn' (*Financial Mail*, South Africa);

'Anglican Church says overpopulation may break eighth commandment' (*The Age*, Australia);

'The population time-bomb is a myth' (*Independent*, Britain).

In spite of this outpouring, which has been building momentum in recent years, it is still claimed that population is a 'taboo' subject that 'nobody' is prepared to discuss. 'Why don't you deal with the

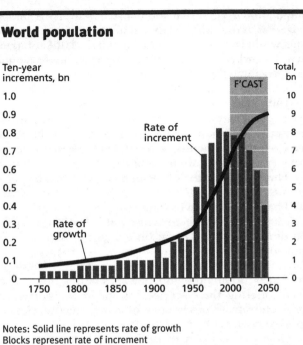

World population

Ten-year increments, bn / Total, bn

F'CAST

Rate of increment

Rate of growth

1750 1800 1850 1900 1950 2000 2050

Notes: Solid line represents rate of growth
Blocks represent rate of increment
One reason the rate of increment is declining is because the fertility rate is falling.

Warning: UN demographers currently offer eight variant projections for the future, with the median (just over 9 billion) being the most cited. All projections are conditional assessments based on current numbers, age structure and trends and reasonable assumptions about the future. This 2050 projection ranges from slightly under 8 billion to slightly over 11 billion.

Source: United Nations Department of Social and Economic Affairs – Population Division, World Population Prospects: the 2008 Revision

real problem?' readers, listeners and high-profile campaigners complain, 'which is overpopulation'.

What are we to make of this? To try to find out I headed for the Moroccan city of Marrakech and the 16th International Population Conference of the International Union of the Scientific Study of

Are too many people being born?

Population (IUSSP). It's the main body that brings together those who study population trends around the world and I understand around 2,000 of them will be gathered there. I'm hoping they might be able to shed some light.

Fertility dips

Two small boys are picking olives off a tree in the central reservation on the road leading to the Palais de Congrès in downtown Marrakech where the week-long conference is about to begin.

The boys place the olives in a bag before moving on to the next tree.

That's it! That's what's missing. Small boys!

I had been trying to work out why Morocco felt so different on this occasion compared with my two previous visits to the country. The first, in 1975, left me with a memory of being constantly besieged by gangs of small – and not so small – boys. They were offering their services as guides or porters or protectors from other boys offering their services as guides, porters or protectors...

On my second visit, in 1987, I was doing a feature for the United Nations Population Fund (UNFPA) which involved following the story of a woman who had just gone into labor. Back in her village a couple of days after the birth, the young mother still looked exhausted. She said she did not want any more children. Five was enough. 'She seems quite determined,' I commented to the midwife who had arranged the visit. She shrugged. 'Maybe. But her husband wants to have more. It's a question of status for him.'

Since then, Morocco has experienced a sharp decline in its fertility rate. Instead of women having seven or eight children, as they did in the 1960s and 1970s, they now have between two and three.

I flick though the two fat booklets provided for the population conference. There are hundreds of sessions on many different aspects of the subject. But there seems to be little relating to a global population explosion. Are these researchers living in a bubble? Don't they hear the raised voices of concern outside their discipline?

As I continue looking, though, I see that from midweek onwards there are some sessions on the link between population and environment.

But for the moment, the issue of 'total fertility rate' – that is how many children women have during the span of their reproductive lives – seems to be the focus of attention.

Since the 1970s, fertility has declined considerably,

The jargon

Demographic transition
When child mortality declines, couples eventually have fewer children, but the transition will usually take at least a generation. In the time it takes for the birth rate to get into balance with the death rate, the population may rise sharply. Demographers call this evolution 'demographic transition'. It's not a universal rule, however.

Demographic dividend
Countries can benefit from certain demographic changes. For example, when the birth rate falls, school rolls follow, educational resources are not so over-stretched, and there is more money available per child for education. Or when a generation of baby boomers finish their education and enter the workforce, there is a sudden influx of economically active rather than dependent people which may help a country develop.

Total fertility rate
This is the average number of children a woman would expect to bear in her lifetime.

Replacement fertility rate
This measures the number of children each woman would need to have to replace a country's population. The current rate is 2.1 children per woman in a fairly affluent country but it may need to be higher than that in a poorer one with a higher mortality rate. So, for example, 2.5 would be a more accurate rate for South Africa. ■

not just in countries like Morocco but worldwide. This makes for a global average of around 2.5 children per women.

In 76 countries the fertility rate has actually sunk below replacement level – which is set at around 2.1. This means the current population is not reproducing itself. About half the world's people live in countries where this has already happened. It's most noticeable in Europe but there are examples from every continent, including Africa.[2]

In 'developing' or Majority World countries the average fertility rate fell by half, from six to three children, between 1950 and 2000. In 31 of these countries the total fertility rate is estimated to have dropped below replacement level.[3] But in sub-Saharan Africa women are still having five or more children on average. This last fact is often cited as evidence that the world's population is still 'exploding'.

But Hania Zlotnik, Director of the UN's Population Division, comments: 'At this moment, much as I want to say there's still a problem of high fertility rates, it's only about 16 per cent of the world population, mostly in Africa.'[4]

It should also be pointed out, though, that in the 17 sub-Saharan nations where birth rates are highest, life expectancy is 50 years or less.

The UN projects that the world will reach replacement fertility by 2030 and dip below replacement at 2.0 children per woman by 2045-50. 'The population as a whole is on a path toward non-explosion – which is good news,' Zlotnik says.[4]

The rate of population growth is likely to be highest in Africa. By 2050 its population is expected to have doubled. In terms of the big global numbers, however, what happens in India and China, the two most populous countries, has the greatest impact. India today has a fertility rate of 2.7 (down from 3.5 in 1997) and is expected to hit replacement level in

2027. China's drop from 5 or 6 per woman before 1970 to around 1.5 today looks likely to persist. 'The accumulated evidence suggests that lifting the one-child policy would not lead to a resurgence of uncontrollable population growth,' say researchers from the region. China, they say, 'would benefit from learning from its neighbors, Korea and Japan, how difficult it is to induce people to increase childbearing once fertility has fallen to a very low level.'[5] As a consequence, China's population should start shrinking by 2023.

According to the United Nations, 21 countries

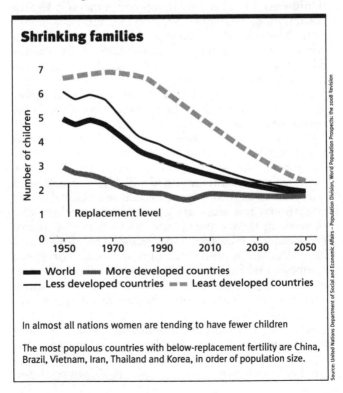

Shrinking families

Number of children

■■ World ▪▪▪ More developed countries
— Less developed countries ▪▪ Least developed countries

In almost all nations women are tending to have fewer children

The most populous countries with below-replacement fertility are China, Brazil, Vietnam, Iran, Thailand and Korea, in order of population size.

Source: United Nations Department of Social and Economic Affairs – Population Division, World Population Prospects: the 2008 Revision

already had declining populations in the period 2000-2005. A further 45 are expected to shrink by at least 10 per cent between 2010 and 2050. Many of these countries are in Europe but they also include populous countries like the US, Russia and Japan.[2]

Chickens and eggs

The rapid expansion of family planning and contraceptive use around the world is one reason for this decline in fertility. Population worriers make much of the projection of nine billion by 2050. But were it not for three decades of successful family planning that figure would be closer to 16 billion, points out leading Australian demographer Peter McDonald.

In Morocco, for example, only five per cent of women used contraception in the late 1970s – today 63 per cent do.[6] But another crucial factor is the progress made in getting girls into school. This, more than anything, delays childbearing, encourages greater spacing between children or even opens up the option of not having children at all.

It's the perfect chicken and egg. Education means lower fertility – and lower fertility can mean more education. One of the immediate benefits of the so-called 'demographic dividend' that comes with fewer children being born is that school rolls fall, educational resources are not so over-stretched, and there is, in theory at any rate, more money available per child for education. In practice the money may be wasted or misdirected. But in South Korea, for example, where the demographic dividend was invested in education, the results in terms of economic and social development over the past few decades have been astounding.

The same felicitous connection exists between health provision and fertility rates. Statistically, a child's chance of survival improves hugely in a smaller family where resources – both physical and emotional – tend to be more concentrated. And if children have a better chance of surviving, their parents will not feel they need to have so many. The flipside of this is that the countries where there is the greatest poverty – those of sub-Saharan Africa, for example – are also those where women both have the most children and lose the most children as infants.

No sex please, we're Japanese

At lunch I get talking with a researcher from Italy, which (at 1.4) has one of the lowest fertility rates in western Europe. She tells me: 'The traditional idea of motherhood is still very strong in Italy. Modern women who work and have careers don't want to be sucked into all that. They do not get enough support, from either the state or their partners, to be able to work and have children.'

In Japan, too, a growing number of women are childless – hence a national fertility rate of just 1.2.

Young Japanese women are better educated than their mothers and have more career opportunities. In spite of this, traditional, patriarchal family values prevail. Though there is a 'departure from marriage' and a third of marriages end in divorce, cohabitation is still frowned upon, as is having children out of wedlock. The rate of 'celibacy' is high for both sexes, compared with the West.

In South Korea the taboo against unmarried women having children is so strong that the overwhelming majority seek abortion or adoption. A woman who chooses to go ahead with a pregnancy and, worse still, keep her child is socially ostracized. She may lose her job, be rejected by her family and will be denied state benefits available to other parents.

Despite such harsh attitudes towards single mothers, policy-makers in the region are getting anxious about falling fertility. According to Noriko Tsuya of Japan's Keio University: 'The Government   has promised

Are too many people being born?

to beef up child allowance but so far attempts to encourage people to have children are not really helping.'

The anxiety is partly fueled by national, cultural and psychological fears. 'A population in decline suggests decay,' observes demographer Paul Demeny of the Population Council, a leading research body. 'It is associated with the collapse of ancient civilizations.'[7] Perhaps a smaller population will reduce a country's clout on the world stage, the thinking goes. Or it might slow down economic growth.

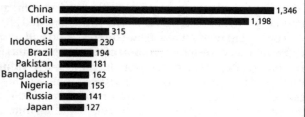

The top 10 most populous countries (in millions)

China — 1,346
India — 1,198
US — 315
Indonesia — 230
Brazil — 194
Pakistan — 181
Bangladesh — 162
Nigeria — 155
Russia — 141
Japan — 127

Source: UNICEF The State of the World's Children 2011

Future growth

During 2010-2050, nine countries are expected to account for half of the world's projected population increase: India, Pakistan, Nigeria, Ethiopia, the US, DR Congo, Tanzania, China and Bangladesh, listed according to the size of their contribution to global population growth.

Future decline

During 2010-2050, 45 countries are expected to decrease in population size. They include Belarus, Bosnia-Herzegovina, Bulgaria, Croatia, Cuba, Georgia, Germany, Greenland, Guyana, Hungary, Japan, Latvia, Lithuania, Niue, Poland, Moldova, Romania, Russia, Ukraine.

Source: UNPD, World Population Prospects: the 2008 Revision, 2009

But even Japan's pronounced fertility decline is 'far from cataclysmic', according to Demeny. The country's population is set to dip from 127 to 102 million in 2050 – still higher than its 1950 figure of 82 million.

For Demeny, the global trend towards falling fertility means 'we are moving towards negative rates of growth, and stabilization at a lower population size.'[7]

Numbers

But how does that tally with growing numbers of people in the world? Remember that median projection of nine billion by 2050 or earlier?

One effect of falling fertility is that our current population growth is temporary. According to the UN projections, world population peaks at about 9.2 billion around mid-century, then declines and stabilizes. That's not to brush aside environmental concerns or the need for treating population projections with caution. But it does put into perspective the alarmist claims of runaway population growth or even an explosion. In terms of birth rates, the main baby booms are already over.

It is true that world population will continue to grow over the next three decades, and that will put pressure on resources, both natural and social. If we don't make significant changes, it will multiply the damage we are already doing to the planet. We have problems, as climate change is now telling us, and we look at how population relates to this in Chapter 7.

But, for those who feel that the planet is too small for us all, it's worth noting that you could fit all the people in the world today in an area the size of Texas and they could live there with the population density currently enjoyed by the citizens of New York.[3]

And while the idea of a population 'time-bomb'

Ten is too many

Vigorously bucking the global trend is the small Indian Ocean state of Timor-Leste. At 7.8 children per woman, Asia's newest nation has the world's highest fertility rate. Some locals blame the island's coffee, which they liken to Viagra. But there are other reasons why the Timorese are having babies like there's no tomorrow.

Up until 1999 the country was brutally occupied by Indonesia, which forced family planning upon the people. Some 102,000 Timorese lost their lives due to conflict during the occupation and many went into exile, leaving behind the poorest and least educated.

During the course of his research, demographer Udoy Saikia of Flinders University in Adelaide, Australia, found that men on the island wanted numerous children and would not hear of family planning. 'There is,' says Saikia, 'something of a psychology that they have to replace people who died.' One man told him: 'Look at that hill. That hill used to be full before. It is empty now.'

The society remains highly patriarchal. Decisions about desirable family size are left to men and 80 per cent of women don't use contraception.

'In the fields I asked women how many children they wanted to have. "My mother said I must have many because I am the only girl in my family," came one reply.' Another was told by her grandparents that she must have nine children. This is in a country where one fifth of the population lives below the poverty line.*

Saikia relates: 'I asked one of the men how many children he had.
"Three," he said.
How many would like to have?
"Seven," the man replied.
Joking, I asked: Why not 10?
He answered: "I'm not employed. I have no income How can you think about 10?"' ∎

* The countries with the fastest-growing populations are often the poorest. Afghanistan, Burkina Faso, Niger, Somalia, and Uganda as well as Timor-Leste are projected to increase their populations by 150 per cent between 2010 and 2050.

Source: 'The world's highest fertility in Asia's newest nation: an investigation into reproductive behaviour of Women in Timor-Leste', by Udoy Saikia, Gouranga Dasvarma, Tanya Wells Brown, IUSSP, 2009.

appeals to excitable headline writers and celebrities corralled to the cause, it pushes few buttons for demographers. In the words of one, 'it's a bit passé'. They seem far more interested in falling fertility and one of its already visible effects – the changing age structure of populations, with fewer people who are young and more who are old.

We come to this in Chapter 3. But first, a look at the chequered history of population concern and control.

1 Carl Haub, '2010 World Population Datasheet', Population Reference Bureau 2010. 2 United Nations Department of Social and Economic Affairs – Population Division (UNPD), *World Population Prospects: the 2008 Revision*, New York 2009. 3 UNPD, *World Population Ageing 2009*, New York 2009. 4 Robert Kunzig, 'Population 7 Billion', *National Geographic*, Jan 2011. 5 Noriko Tsuya, Minja Kim Choe, Wang Fen, 'Below Replacement Fertility in East Asia: Patterns, Factors and Policy Implications', paper for IUSSP, Marrakech 2009. 6 Therese Locoh/Zahia Oudah-Bedidi, poster session at IUSSP, Marrakech 2009. 7 Session at IUSSP, Marrakech 2009.

2 A brief history of population

The story of counting people and trying to control fertility is intense and mixed, with episodes of both radical liberation and brutal coercion. Racism, class prejudice, sexism and eugenics have all had roles to play in its murkiest moments.

BEFORE THE DEVELOPMENT of agriculture in around 10,000 BCE, the world is believed to have had a population of about one million. Fast forward to 400 BCE and the idea of 'population control' made an appearance in Plato's *Republic*, which proposed that the 'guardian' class could be bred to rule, with the 'unfit ' left to die. By 300-400 CE, the combined eastern and western Roman empire alone numbered around 55 million people. Recurrent plagues halved Europe's population between 541 and 750. By 1340 world population had risen again to more than 440 million, but so devastating was the Black Death that by 1400 human numbers had dropped by nearly a quarter. (It would take roughly 200 years for Europe to regain its 1340 level.) During the Middle Ages, Ibn Khaldun (1332-1406), a North African polymath, produced the first scientific and theoretical work on population, development and group dynamics – the *Muqaddimah*.

After 1400 world population grew more steadily. One reason was food. New crops that had come from the Americas to Asia and Europe during the 16th century contributed to population growth on these continents. The indigenous populations of the Americas, however, were decimated by diseases brought by European colonizers. During the agricultural and industrial revolutions in Europe, child life expectancy improved dramatically. The percentage of children born in London who died before the age of five decreased from 74.5 per cent in 1730-49 to 31.8 per cent in

1810-29. Europe's population doubled to almost 200 million during the 18th century, and doubled again during the 19th century, thanks to improved living conditions and healthcare. But Europe's gain was Asia's and Africa's loss, as colonial exploitation continued to cause poverty and hunger. Between 1877 and 1902 India and China alone had suffered 30 to 60 million deaths from famine.

Enter Thomas Robert Malthus

At the end of the 18th century, a Church of England curate and mathematician of the land-owning classes, Thomas Robert Malthus, concluded that, if unchecked, populations would be subject to exponential growth. His influential 1798 *Essay on the Principle of Population* argued that population growth would outstrip growth in food production, leading to ever-increasing famine and poverty. He based this on the assertion that population grows 'geometrically' – the larger the base of population the larger the increase with no 'effort' needed. Food production, meanwhile, grows in a slower 'arithmetic' way – each incremental increase requiring the same extra effort no matter how much food was produced to start with. The result, he argued, was that populations would outrun food production, until famine or the misery of war restored the balance.

Events in his own lifetime proved him wrong: population continued increasing but so did food production, thanks to improvements in agriculture. His pessimistic view was a reaction against Enlightenment thinkers Antoine-Nicolas Cordorcet and William Godwin who had argued that social misery was caused by defective institutions and could be addressed by reform. Malthus reckoned that poverty was a simple and natural consequence of population growth – not of inequality. Welfare measures merely intensified impoverishment since they allowed the poor to breed more.

During the period of industrial expansion Europe's population increased rapidly. This was often considered a good thing by governments and opinion-makers, who associated prosperity and military security with growing numbers. Racial and Darwinian thinking encouraged the idea that the presumed 'superior' and 'fittest' people would flourish and grow. But the British privileged classes noticed – and became obsessively concerned – that the 'unfit' lower social classes seemed to be reproducing even faster than they were.

For heterosexually active people of any class fertility was a mixed blessing. In Britain during the 19th century the average age of marriage declined and the number of children per woman rose – and with it the risk of death in childbirth. In the latter part of the century, 1 in 200 births was fatal for the mother. Among the upper classes one in ten babies perished before their first birthday; in working-class families it was more like one in seven.

In 1877 Annie Besant and Charles Bradlaugh published a pamphlet by Charles Knowlton called *The Fruits of Philosophy*, which advised people on how to have sex without getting pregnant. Methods included condoms, douches, sponges and withdrawal. The devices were hardly new – Casanova had used a condom in 18th-century Venice – but describing them all in one publication was revolutionary. *The Fruits of Philosophy* sold 133,000 copies before Besant and Bradlaugh were put on trial for publishing an 'obscene' pamphlet. The 29-year-old Besant put up a spirited and erudite defense, quoting Malthus, Darwin and Dickens, among others, and arguing that it was a 'crime' against society to bring children into the world for whom one could not provide. She and Bradlaugh were found guilty but released on a legal technicality. Besant went on to publish a pamphlet of her own, *The Law of Population*, in which she insisted that famines – such as those afflicting India and China at the time – were 'caused entirely by overpopulation'. It sold hundreds of thousands of copies and was translated into German, French, Italian and Dutch. Across England the birth rate began to fall – most sharply among professional couples and their domestic servants. The pattern was repeated across much of Europe for the last two decades of the 19th century.

The birth of birth control

On the other side of the Atlantic, in a run-down district of New York, a young girl was observing the toll on her mother of having given birth to 13 children. A few years later, working as a visiting nurse on Manhattan's impoverished Lower East Side, the young Margaret Sanger saw women on the brink of death due to septic abortions. She was determined to do something about it. 'No woman can call herself free who does not own and control her own body,' Sanger was to declare. The 'birth control' movement was born. Opposition was fierce and included the Catholic church. One bishop warned: 'the races from northern Europe... the finest of people... [were] doomed to extinction, unless each family produces at least four children.'

Like Annie Besant before her, Margaret Sanger was no slouch when it came to challenging authority. The Comstock Law prohibited the sale of contraceptives but she openly promoted them in her newspaper *The Woman Rebel*. She further challenged prosecutors by setting up her own birth-control clinic in Brooklyn. Arrested, she refused to be fingerprinted, threatened a hunger strike and spent 30 days in jail.

Sanger was operating in a period where pro-natalism was at its height. The 1914-18 World War, and the flu pandemic that immediately followed it, had claimed millions of young lives, prompting nationalist calls for patriotic families to have more children.

In Italy there were harsh penalties for anyone

interfering with the social duty to add to the nation's stock. At the same time, the 'science' of eugenics was taking off on both sides of the Atlantic. Sanger, like fellow campaigner Marie Stopes in Britain, was caught up in the eugenicist agenda to 'improve' the human race. Eugenicists had long been critical of the indiscriminate promotion of birth control because they said it was reducing the fertility only of women who were educated enough to use it. Marie Stopes reassured them: 'Constructive Birth Control will fill the comfortable cradles, and empty the gutters.' Sanger was more explicit, saying: 'There has never been any birth control movement that did not lay stress on the eugenics side of it.'

Eugenics triumphs

In the US, racist fears that black people might be breeding faster than whites and that immigrants from China and elsewhere were 'overwhelming' the Anglo-Saxon population became widespread in the early 20th century. Campaigners wanted immigration control, fearing the 'extinction of the Mayflower descendants'. In 1924 the Natural Origins Act barred immigrants and also expelled many who were not white. Eugenicists also won the passage of a compulsory sterilization law. By 1931 California had sterilized 7,500 people deemed unfit to reproduce.

Racially inspired population policies were popping up in other parts of the world. In 1936 Soviet officials withdrew contraceptives from the market, made abortion illegal and offered mothers cash payments to bear large families, while deporting entire ethnic groups considered 'un-Soviet'.

Meanwhile, in Britain, imperialists argued that the maintenance of the Empire required a steady increase in the population of the 'English' race. Such concern led to the establishment of the Royal Commission on Population in 1937. When the British Eugenics

Society set up its Population Policies Committee in 1938, the aim was not to increase fertility at random but to 'improve [the] reproductive power of the eugenically good'.

But the country that took 'population control' to its cruellest extremes was Germany. Back in 1905, eugenicists had formed the German Society for Racial Hygiene. Before Hitler came to power in 1933, diverse social movements had pushed for pro-natalism, improved healthcare, eugenics and sex reform. The Nazis used these ideas and pressed them into the service of racial purity and antisemitism.

Under Hitler, groups were empowered to implement eugenic matchmaking, massive sterilization programs and the secret killing of disabled people. 'Hitler would explain the conquest, depopulation and resettlement of eastern Europe as "the planned control of population movements to restore the numbers and quality of the Aryan race",' writes historian Matthew Connelly.

The horrors of Nazism, and the role that eugenics played in the murder of millions of Jews, Roma, disabled and homosexual people, meant that after the Second World War such views were less popular or explicitly expressed. But eugenicist thinking and practice persisted. In the US and Scandinavia, programs to sterilize people – whether for 'feeblemindedness' or anti-social behavior – accelerated. Post-war eugenic sterilization laws were passed with ease in Denmark, Norway, Sweden and Finland.

Booming babies
While the Second World War was claiming millions of lives, it was also bringing many millions more into being. In Japan, for example, the population grew by 2.5 million people between 1940 and 1945. Soon a post-war baby boom was echoing around the world. Birth rates increased rapidly in the US, Britain and the Commonwealth countries.

A brief history of population

Population was growing – but not just because of new babies. War-time food rations had paradoxically improved the general state of nutrition in many cases, while the development of antibiotic drugs, vaccines and pesticides were adding five million people who would have otherwise died. Though later rejected for its harmful side-effects, DDT was highly effective in reducing deaths from malaria across the world.

In 1947 the United Nations Population Commission met for the first time. Concern about population had become global and with it the sense that something could be done at a global, international level. Margaret Sanger and others involved in the 'birth control' movement were able to secure generous funding for their campaign work, which took off around the world.

The UN was now gathering more precise figures on population growth in Asia, Africa and Latin America. At the same time, colonial powers were beginning to lose their hold in these areas. One British governor in Kenya insisted that high fertility and poverty would drive unrest in the colony. The French authorities were warned that the 'decisive problem' in colonial Algeria was 'a demographic one'.

Population growth was being described as an 'explosion'. Neo-Malthusian worries about food scarcity resurfaced. Now the people deemed to be 'breeding too fast' were those in the so-called Third World. By 1956 US sociologist JO Hertzler was writing: 'These people are problems, even hazards, for all those countries of the world... as areas of economic dependence, as explosive centers of unrest and as possible disturbers of world peace.'

In 1958, Yale University demographers Ansley Coale and Edgar Hoover produced a seminal thesis that rapid population growth had a negative impact on economic development. India had by then become the first country to adopt a formal population policy, though by 1958 it was still fairly ineffectual. That year Sweden's government became the first to include family planning in its foreign aid budget. The US followed suit with big money for countries prepared to commit to programs to reduce their birth rates. For some countries, Bangladesh for instance, such commitments were to become a condition for foreign aid and even loans from the World Bank being granted.

'The Population Bomb'

During this Cold War period 'strategic demography' was taking off, with experts examining population growth in terms of security risk. One specific fear was that the burgeoning yet impoverished South might be inclined to communism. Population was growing fastest in Asia and John Robbins' 1959 book *Too Many Asians* was typical of the period. For him, the Indian state of Kerala exemplified the problem: this populous state had just elected a communist government. Paul Ehrlich's 1968 best-seller, *The Population Bomb*, warned of mass starvation. Like those of his predecessor, Malthus, Ehrlich's dire predictions did not materialize. But his book was highly influential, nonetheless.

Its opening chapter set the tone for an era. Describing his arrival by taxi on a 'hot stinking night' in Delhi, Ehrlich wrote: 'As we crawled through the city, we entered a crowded slum... the streets seemed alive with people. People eating, people washing, people sleeping, people visiting, arguing and screaming. People thrusting their hands through the taxi window, begging. People defecating and urinating... People, people, people, people.'

Ehrlich called for population control everywhere. In the US, it should be done through incentives and penalties – and through compulsion if these methods failed. In poor countries and communities, it would be

A brief history of population

a condition of receiving food aid.

When Ehrlich went to India, to study butterflies, he seemed unaware that the country was already in the throes of a controversial drive to reduce births, through sterilization and insertion of inter-uterine-devices (IUDs). The US-based Population Council had sent one million IUDs to India, before a factory was built to produce them locally.

Big financial incentives came to the Indian government through USAID, the World Bank, the Ford Foundation and the UN. Together, these organizations provided most of India's $1.5-billion aid package. Cash incentives were offered not only to men who would accept vasectomies but also to family-planning staff and motivators. The poorest people were the main targets – during a famine in Bihar, hundreds of thousands came forward to be sterilized in exchange for cash.

Meanwhile, the IUDs being provided to Indian women were causing infection: 28 per cent of 13-24 year olds fitted with an IUD had to have the device removed before a year was up due to excessive bleeding.

When Indira Gandhi came to power in 1966, she was determined to give family planning a higher priority. She herself had nearly died after the birth of her second son, Sanjay. But, ironically perhaps, it was Sanjay she put in charge of the program that was to be her political undoing. In 1976 Gandhi used state of emergency powers to force a dramatic increase in sterilizations. From 1976 to 1977 the number of operations tripled, to more than eight million – six million vasectomies and two million tubectomies.

Family-planning workers were pressured to meet quotas; in some states, sterilization was a condition for receiving new housing or other government benefits. There were cases of police rounding up poor people and taking them to sterilization camps. Foreign donors responded not by withdrawing funding but by increasing it. Sanjay Gandhi's population policy, combined with his ruthless slum-clearance policy, outraged the Indian people, however. In the general elections that followed, Indira Gandhi was ousted from power.

Particularly controversial had been the fact that men were targeted – yet the sterilization of women was still promoted. Women continued to be seen as the cause of the population 'problem'.

China's one-child policy

During the 1970s, population became an increasingly politicized subject. Controversy raged; consensus was rare. Was high population growth the chief obstacle to development or was poverty at the root of population problems? And who had the right to say whether a woman should or should not have children?

Feminists like Germaine Greer openly challenged the patriarchal orthodoxy that had ruled policy-makers, population professionals and demographers – in spite of the existence of leading women campaigners like Margaret Sanger, Marie Stopes and Elise Ottesen-Jensen.

At the stormy World Population Conference in Bucharest in 1974, the main message to emerge was that 'development is the best contraceptive'. The following two decades saw a rapid expansion of access to family-planning services on all continents, with a widening range of technologies available. But coercive practices in Bangladesh and Indonesia, as well as India, continued to undermine public confidence, arouse suspicion and give family planning a bad name.

The most extreme experiment in population control was yet to come, however.

It all started in 1978 when Chinese missile scientist Jian Song went to a conference in Helsinki and learned about a team from the Massachusetts Institute of Technology that was running simulations to model the effects of increasing population and resource use. The results were published as a report, *The Limits to Growth*, which warned of overshoot, collapse and exhaustion of all known oil reserves by 1992. When Song and his team ran the calculations through computers to predict China's future, they concluded that if Chinese women had an average of three children the population would grow to four billion by 2080. This spelt doom. If China did not reduce its fertility to 1.5 or even one child per woman, the resulting depletion of resources would be disastrous. Conversely, if it were able to contain this growth, China could become prosperous.

Actually the fertility rate in China was already going down – it had decreased from 6.4 to 2.7 over the previous decade. But Song convinced China's leadership to launch a campaign to halt all population growth by the year 2000.

The first step was to collect data. China asked for international assistance with improving data and obtaining computers to process it. Brigades, production teams and street committee leaders were instructed to monitor women of childbearing years. Some officials made women submit to monthly gynecological exams. Women who opted for an abortion earned 14 days' paid vacation – 40 days if it occurred in the second trimester and was quickly followed by sterilization. Incentives included subsidies for only one child, priority in housing and extra retirement pay. But parents who then had a second child would have to repay these benefits. Those who had more than two would have their pay docked by 10 per cent for 14 years.

Rural areas, where bearing a son was viewed as crucial, were hard to monitor. So the authorities launched crash drives with shock teams led by senior officials who went from village to village. Failing cadres were humiliated, offenders isolated. Pregnant women – even those beyond five months – were forced to undergo abortion by caesarean section. Using these methods, in 1979 China was able to register 7.9 million abortions, 13.5 million IUD insertions, and almost 7 million sterilizations.

Although reports of these abuses were beginning to reach the West, family-planning bodies such as the UN Population Fund (UNFPA) kept funding China's program, with generous help from Japan. In 1980 staff at the International Planned Parenthood Federation (IPPF) became concerned after the BBC reported cases of abortions being conducted on women eight months pregnant, of women committing suicide and of attacks on prospective parents. China's one-child policy also had a eugenic hue, with discussion of measures to prevent reproduction among those likely to pass on defects, 'including bisexuality'.

The measures became more coercive. All women with one child were to be fitted with a stainless steel, tamper-resistant IUD; all parents with two or more children were to be sterilized; and all unauthorized pregnancies were to be aborted. In 1983 more than 16 million women and more than 4 million men were sterilized, nearly 18 million women were inserted with IUDs and 14 million underwent abortions.

One of the most tragic consequences of China's draconian one-child policy was the rising number of infant girls being killed by their parents due to the traditional preference for sons. In 1983, after years of resistance in rural areas, officials relaxed the rules to allow people who had one daughter to try for a son. With the arrival of ultrasound technology, people were able to sex-select and abort female fetuses, with the result that many more boys were being born. The usual rate of 6 per cent more boys had leapt to 17 per cent by 1995.

The international population establishment failed

to speak up for the human rights of Chinese citizens. It continued to grant financial support in spite of evidence of mass coercion. This played straight into the hands of religious and other opponents to abortion, contraception and family planning. The Vatican – opposed to contraception as well as abortion – claimed the moral high ground, as did Protestant evangelical

---

A tale of two policies

IRAN
Achieved the fastest fertility decline in the world, from 6.6 children per woman in 1970 to 1.9 today.

How did they do it?
The country's religious leaders who came to power in the 1979 Revolution were pro-natalist and abolished the beginnings of a family-planning system. Soldiers were needed for the war with Iraq. But in 1989, after the end of the war, a major policy change took place. Iranian population experts managed to convince the religious leadership that very high fertility rates were no longer in the interests of the country.

The government mobilized a comprehensive 'quality of life' campaign, with family-planning classes for all and free contraception. Women as well as men were given condoms.

The campaign coincided with a dramatic increase in the educational level of younger women, especially in the rural areas. In 1976 only 10 per cent of rural women aged 20 to 24 were literate. This increased to 37 per cent in 1986, then 78 per cent in 1996 and by 2006 it was 91 per cent.

Farzaneh Roudi, of the Population Reference Bureau, comments: 'People outside Iran imagine that the family-planning program must have been coercive but it wasn't. There was widespread public education about family planning; everyone was talking about it. Women had more control over their own fertility than in the time of the Shah. And it didn't lead to many more boys being born than girls, as in some other countries.'

CHINA
Launched the world's most radical population policy, which is credited with bringing down the fertility rate from 5-6 children per woman in 1970 to an estimated 1.5 today.

How did they do it?
China's national family planning program began in earnest in 1971 with the *wan xi shao* policy which advocated later marriage, longer birth intervals and fewer children. In 1979 the Government introduced a

---

groups with similar objections. The UNFPA, IPPF and USAID were targeted, with some success; aid grants were cut and department heads lost their jobs.

Women to the rescue

The religious lobby was powerful, rich and influential – especially in the US.

radical population program with the 'one-child family' policy at its heart. Enforcement was tightened up in 1981 in urban areas and in 1982 in rural parts. Severe human rights abuses occurred, including forced abortions (see page 33). The policy was relaxed in the mid-1980s through the 'one small hole' shift which enabled couples in rural areas whose first child was a girl to have a second child. But it was tightened in 1988 and again in the 1990s.

Today, despite having achieved below replacement fertility for over a decade, two-thirds of Chinese parents may only have one child. Parents who don't comply are punished. So are local cadres, whose performance is linked to achievement of target fertility in their local area. Failure may cost wages or even dismissal. This, together with the complications of monitoring internal migration, is probably leading to some under-reporting of births. But the current 1.5 fertility rate estimate takes account of this.

The one-child policy has been blamed for skewing sex ratios. In 1963 the ratio was 104 boys to 100 girls born; by 2007 it was 120 to 100. Yuhua Yang of the Renmin University of China, says: 'We need to ban sex-selective abortion.' But she is not convinced that the one-child policy is the cause of imbalance. Rather, this exacerbates a cultural preference for sons. She advocates more profound change to address this: 'We need to tackle gender inequality and to develop need-specific policies to give preference to females.'

Question: *Would China have achieved its birth-rate decline if it had adopted a policy that was more like Iran's and not so coercive?*
Many experts – including Chinese demographers – think it would have. As people became richer and girls became better educated, people would have voluntarily elected to have fewer children, as they have done in other countries, such as Japan and Korea.

Question: *Is China likely to give up its one-child policy?*
Many Chinese demographers are advocating that it should do so. The rule has been relaxed in Shanghai recently. ∎

Source: *New Internationalist*, 'When sperm didn't meet ovum', Jan/Feb 2010

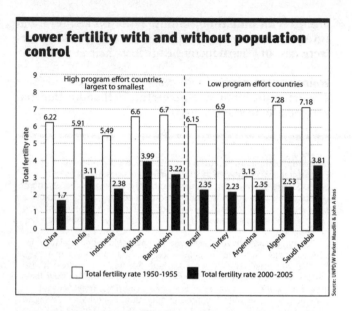

Lower fertility with and without population control

High program effort countries, largest to smallest

Low program effort countries

Total fertility rate

China: 6.22 / 1.7
India: 5.91 / 3.11
Indonesia: 5.49 / 2.38
Pakistan: 6.6 / 3.99
Bangladesh: 6.7 / 3.22
Brazil: 6.15 / 2.35
Turkey: 6.9 / 2.23
Argentina: 3.15 / 2.35
Algeria: 7.28 / 2.53
Saudi Arabia: 7.18 / 3.81

☐ Total fertility rate 1950-1955   ■ Total fertility rate 2000-2005

Source: UNPD/W Parker Maudlin & John A Ross

But another force had emerged that would oppose it every inch of the way: second-wave feminism.

From the mid-1960s, the oral contraceptive pill, though originally intended for Majority World use, had helped bring about a sexual revolution in the West. Women had greater freedom than ever before to have sex with men *and* pursue educational, professional and other activities. They were delaying having children or even choosing not to have them at all. Feminist thinking and activism was flourishing; its effects reaching far and wide. One result, quite naturally, was a fall in birth rates. In the US, fertility – which had peaked in 1957 at 123 births per 1,000 women aged 15-44 – had fallen to just 65 by 1976.

The women's health movement was coming into its own. 'Population Control No!' was the slogan of the Women's International Tribunal and Meeting on Reproductive Rights, where 400 women came together to condemn both population control and anti-abortion forces. In 1984 the Women's Global Network of Reproductive Rights was set up. A year later, at the UN World Conference of Women in Nairobi, feminist activists were to propose and have accepted the first UN statement that recognized not only that women had 'the basic right to control their own fertility' but that this was the basis for all other rights. US activist Betsy Hartmann's book *Reproductive Rights and Wrongs* exposed population control's long history of mistreatment of women and added to the rising clamor for a rights-based approach to family planning and its separation from population ideology.

In 1987, a female Pakistani doctor, Nafiz Sadik, took over as head of the UNFPA. She demanded voluntary programs and threatened to withdraw funding from those subject to national policies, quotas and penalties. Family planning was to be about reproduction and health and not just a means of population control.

In the words of historian Matthew Connelly: 'Feminist critics of population control, long marginalized and belittled, ridiculed and harassed, would finally redeem the cause of reproductive rights, and not a moment too soon.'

In September 1994 the United Nations co-ordinated an International Conference on Population and Development in Cairo. The agenda focused on women's empowerment. Despite fierce opposition from Christian and Muslim religious conservatives, the conference achieved consensus on the following four goals: universal primary education and women's access to education and training; significant reduction of infant and under-five mortality; reduction of maternal mortality to half the 1990 levels by 2000 and half that again by 2015; access to a wide range of reproductive and sexual health services, including family planning, and active discouragement of female genital mutilation.

But the Cairo consensus came in for some scathing criticism from leading women's groups in India who saw it as pushing through a western agenda. 'Surely it is significant,' writes Indian health expert and academic Mohan Rao, 'that the Cairo consensus not only had the imprimatur of the World Bank, but was silent on what the Bank had unleashed on women and their rights and entitlements globally, through structural adjustment programs?'

Meanwhile, criticism of decisions made at Cairo was was soon to come from quite another quarter. The Religious Right was back again with traditionalists in the US administration of George W Bush forcing through drastic cuts in funding for family planning – to be reversed again by President Obama's 2008/09 budget.

Today, concerns about biological limits to growth – that were already being expressed in the 1980s – have resurfaced with renewed vigor. Climate change has added urgency to debates on population and the environmental limits to growth. 'Population control' is back on the agenda of certain campaign groups.

This chapter draws extensively from the work of Matthew Connelly and Betsy Hartmann.
Sources: Matthew Connelly, *Fatal Misconception*, Belknap Harvard, 2008; Betsy Hartmann, *Reproductive Rights and Wrongs*, Southend Press 1995. Robert Engelman, *More*, Island Press, 2008; Larry Lohmann, 'Re-Imagining the Population Debate', Corner House, 2003; Frank Furedi, *Population and Development*, Polity Press, 1997; *New Internationalist*, 'A brief history of population', Jan-Feb 2010.

3 Being alive, staying alive – and growing old

Women are having fewer children. More of them are surviving. People are living longer. As a result, the average age of the world's population is increasing. So is the angst around 'population ageing'...

'HOPE I DIE before I get old,' sang The Who in *My Generation*. Ironically, it is The Who's generation of baby boomers that is proving least likely to die before it grows old.

Since 1950, global average life expectancy has increased by an amazing 21 years – from 46 in 1950-55 to 67 in 2005-10. This scale of generation-upon-generation increase has never been seen before in human history.[1]

At its root lies success. There are few events more tragic than the loss of a child. But in the past 60 years the likelihood of a child dying before the age of five has halved. And the rate of improvement is accelerating all the time. In 1990 almost 90 children per 1,000 did not reach their fifth birthday; by 2008 it was down to 65.[2]

Medical advancements such as the discovery of penicillin, vaccines for polio and treatments for malaria are commonly given as the reasons for this. But far more significant are improvements in nutrition and the standards of living, clean water and public healthcare.

A child's chances of survival still depend far too much upon where in the world she or he is born. But the survival trend is, in most places, going the right way. If parents know their child has a good chance of survival they are less likely to feel the need to have many children, and, as we have seen, children of smaller families have a greater chance of survival. So,

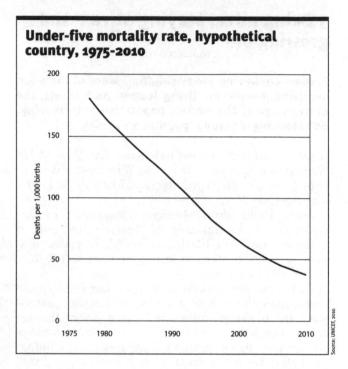

Under-five mortality rate, hypothetical country, 1975-2010

Deaths per 1,000 births

200

150

100

50

0

1975   1980   1990   2000   2010

Source: UNICEF, 2010

fewer children are born but they survive childhood and become adults.

As adults, thanks to better health and diet, they are living longer than their parents and much longer than their grandparents. There's still a large gap between rich and poor when it comes to life expectancy but the sharpest increase has been not, as is often assumed, in industrialized countries, but in the Majority World where people can now expect to live 24 years longer than their compatriots 60 years ago.[1]

Mixed blessings

All these factors put together have had a result that some are seeing as more of a curse than a blessing.

In 2045, for the first time ever, the number of older persons in the world is likely to exceed the number of children – and in many countries this has already happened.

'Can you help me with my guilty conscience?' a Thai family-planning promoter asked fellow population professionals at one of the IUSSP meetings. 'For the past 30 years I have been telling people about the benefits of having fewer children. Now, people are complaining to me that their community is ageing and there are not enough young people.'

'Not enough young people.' It sounds like PD James' futuristic novel *Children of Men* in which, for no explicable reason, babies stop being born.

Already there are examples, mainly in Europe, of ageing ghost towns and villages, where the young and those with qualifications leave as soon as they can to find work in cities or abroad. Towns like Hoyerswerda, close to the Polish border in Germany, which has lost half its population in 20 years and where the remaining residents are not having babies.[3]

Some of the political consequences of ageing populations erupted on the streets of France in 2010 as thousands protested against government plans to increase the retirement age. When state pensions were first introduced, in several Western countries, for men at 65 they were expected to live to 69 or so. Now average life expectancy for men in these countries is 78 or 79 and for women it's around 84.

A major UN population study on the phenomenon of population ageing around the world warns that its effects will reach into all areas of human life and activity. It will affect employment, housing demands, migration trends, healthcare services, savings, pensions, consumption, and transfer of economic resources – not to mention intergenerational relationships.[1]

But there are also a number of assumptions

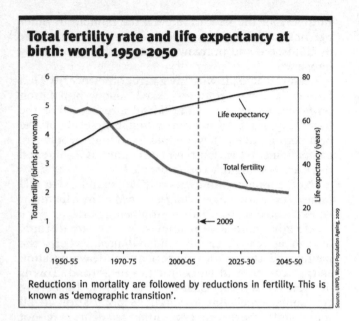

Total fertility rate and life expectancy at birth: world, 1950-2050

Reductions in mortality are followed by reductions in fertility. This is known as 'demographic transition'.

Source: UNPD, World Population Ageing, 2009

and misconceptions flying around that need to be questioned and challenged. Here are a few:

Is it true that....?

'Population ageing is mainly a problem for the rich world'

Not so. Life expectancy may be highest in the richest countries, with Japan topping the list with an average of 83 years, but most old people actually live in the Majority World. Of the world's 529 million over-65s, more than 60 per cent are living in developing countries.[4] In Ghana the number of elderly people has tripled since 1970; by 2012 Shanghai will be the oldest city in the world: it doesn't even have one child per two families.

By mid-century four in five of the world's older people will be living in the Global South. Today,

Europe has the oldest population, with a median age of nearly 40 years that is expected to reach 47 by 2050. But the pervasiveness of population ageing means that, by mid-century, 43 developing countries will also have median ages of higher than 40.[5]

'Population ageing is catastrophic'

In 1950 average life expectancy in Majority World countries was 50 years for men, 53 years for women. In 2010 they were expected to hit 69 and 76 years, respectively. The projections for 2050 are 74 and 80 years.[4] 'Catastrophe' suggests a sudden unpredictable event; the graying of nations is a gradual process. Admittedly, it will happen faster in countries where the fertility decline has been very rapid – and these tend to be in the Global South. But there is at least time to plan. Two things happen when a baby boom ends. In the first stage, there is a 'demographic dividend' when the boomers enter the workforce and are productive without being dependent. In the second stage, those boomers retire – and that is the stage we are entering now. The current 'bulge' – the result of baby boomers hitting old age – will not last for ever and the overall trend of population ageing will settle down to a more gentle increase.

'It burdens younger people'

Demographers and policy-makers talk of the 'dependency ratio' of older, retired citizens to younger, working ones. An OECD report projects that, by 2050, ten 'active workers' will be 'supporting' more than seven older 'inactive people' compared with just four in 2000.[6] But this can be misleading because it leaves dependent children out of the equation. The overall dependency ratio – that is the ratio of 'supporting' people of working age (15-64) to the combined number of 'dependent people', both aged and children – will not increase so dramatically because the

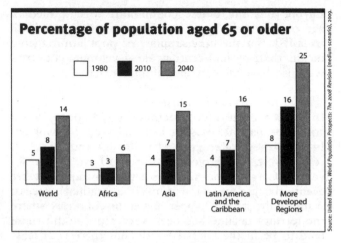

Percentage of population aged 65 or older

□ 1980 ■ 2010 ▨ 2040

World: 5, 8, 14
Africa: 3, 3, 6
Asia: 4, 7, 15
Latin America and the Caribbean: 4, 7, 16
More Developed Regions: 8, 16, 25

Source: United Nations, *World Population Prospects: The 2008 Revision* (medium scenario), 2009.

declining fertility rate means fewer children. In fact, the 'total dependency ratio' remains pretty stable until 2025, at which point it will be 52:100 (that is one person aged under 15 or over 65 to every two people aged 15-64). It will then increase gradually to reach 56:100 by 2050.[1]

Meanwhile, the assumption that people over retirement age are economically 'dependent' on younger working people also needs to be questioned. One fifth of over-65s in the world are still economically active. And while state pension systems tend to be devised in such a way as to make current taxpayers fund entitlements for the current older generation, this is not reflected at a family or community level. Often money goes the other way, from older to younger family members. This is not only true in Western nations, where older people may have accumulated savings or property, but also in Latin America where money tends to flow down the generations, from older to younger. In Asia it is, in theory, common for money to flow upwards from middle-aged workers to their elderly parents. But even in traditional societies, having children to 'keep me in my old age' is often more a saying than a reality. The cost of raising a child usually far exceeds the support a parent may get back in old age, but this is rarely taken into account.

'People living longer has messed up the pensions system'
'In 2050 will there be enough people working to pay for pensions?' asks Frans Willekens, director of the Netherlands Interdisciplinary Demographic Institute in The Hague.[7] The answer is, most likely, 'no'.

Pensions are in crisis – not just in the richer countries but around the world. But the blame lies not with 'too many old people'. It lies with the neoliberal model that allowed and encouraged the financial sector – including pension fund managers – to gamble recklessly with the future economic security of its senior citizens.[8]

The global financial and then economic crisis which erupted in 2008 has hammered pension funds and rates of return on retirement savings. In Australia and Ireland rates of return collapsed by 38 per cent. Losses were heavy too in Belgium, Canada, Hungary, Iceland and the US. Retirees and workers approaching retirement were most severely affected.[1]

The Global South has a pensions crisis of a different sort – for most people a pension is but a dream. Four out of five older people in the world today have no pension provision at all.[1] In Morocco, for example, only one fifth of people aged over 65 get any kind of provision; in Mexico pensions rarely reach those entitled, thanks to pervasive corruption. Political corruption in Latin America has meant that some sectors have won unfair access to pensions at the expense of others. Pensions may be granted at a very early age, after only 10 years' work, with minimal or no contributions at all. This raises pensions costs and creates financially unsustainable schemes that end up paying out little or nothing. Often pensions are available only to workers in urban areas – and even these tend to be very low. However, Brazil has managed to extend minimal assistance to rural workers.

'Ageing impoverishes nations'
In northern European countries with generous welfare arrangements, policy-makers are wondering how to keep the system going. But the contribution of older people to national economies is seldom properly accounted for. Who, for example, is measuring the voluntary work done by retired people? The childcare or other forms of support given by grandparents, great-grandparents or other older family members? If these things were measured, a rather different picture would emerge. Spanish grandparents threatened to go on strike in September 2010 to make this point. In the parts of Africa worst affected by AIDS it is the oldest people – often grandmothers – who are raising orphaned children. In richer countries, older people tend to consume less than younger people but they may need to buy more services. The care services they may require in older years create employment. But in many parts of the world old people are living in poverty and are not getting a fair share of the economic growth that they helped create. Majority World governments could take a leaf out of the book of Bolivian president Evo Morales, who introduced a universal state old-age pension funded by profits from the country's oil and gas wealth. US economics writer Tom Fishman, author of *Shock of Gray*, points to the market opportunities provided by an ageing population 'that is focused on staying healthy and vital'. One of the 'really giant areas', he says, is continuing education.

'Public health costs will rocket thanks to ageing populations'
Analysts are anticipating a massive increase in the cost of caring for people with chronic conditions as a result

McGILL UNIVERSITY BOOKSTORE
LIBRAIRIE UNIVERSITE McGILL
3420 McTAVISH
MONTREAL, QC, H3A 3L1
514-398-7444

Reg_14

Sale   09/04/13 10:23

Receipt: M1432092-14

13Q

1 CHIVERS / NO-NONSENSE GUIDE T   Y $13.95
    12244058
    978-1-897071-71-7
1 HINRICHS / SOCI 250 SOCIAL PR   Y $13.75
    12274901 $27.70
    978-1-4599-1807-8 $1.38
                        Subtotal:

                                          $29.08
                        Total: $29.08
                                          $0.00

Tax:
    GST - 5%

Tender:
    DEBIT CARD

Change Due: THANK YOU
                                          MERCI

GST# 119128992
QST# 1006

Goods ma
    exch

of population ageing. Chronic health conditions such as arthritis and cardiovascular disease do increase with age. However, in terms of health provision, the two years before death are the most costly and living longer does not necessarily add to that.[7] An older person with a healthy lifestyle is likely to make fewer demands on public health services than an unfit middle-aged one. The diseases associated with poor diet, lack of exercise and obesity, are the future health time-bombs. So are diseases associated with stress, deprivation and inequality. These problems are not especially associated with older people but apply across the board. A much stronger link exists between poverty and poor health, than between age and ill-health. So the effort would be better spent on alleviating poverty and improving preventative public health across generations.[1]

Are we prepared?

Even before the current economic crisis there were warning signs that most societies were ill-prepared for population ageing. This is in spite of the fact that demographers have been predicting it since the 1980s.

Now, in the grip of global recession, many countries are hastily rewriting the rules. Some, like Greece, have slashed individual state pensions. Others, like Britain and France, are set to increase the age of retirement.

But in countries where jobs are in short supply and where youth unemployment is a mounting social problem, this is far from ideal. Developing more flexible work cultures with greater opportunity for part-time work and graduated retirement makes more sense.

According to Will Hutton of Britain's Work Foundation, managing the talent of people in their sixties and seventies, together with dealing with the question of fairness in organizations, will be key issues for the world of work in the coming years. The

FACTS: Ageing world

• In 2009, there were 700 million people aged over 60. This is expected to rise to 2,000 million by 2050. The fastest-growing group is the over-80s.
• Whereas the over-65s accounted for, on average, 8% of the world's population in 1950, by 2009 this had gone up to 11% and it is predicted to reach 22% by 2050.
• Life expectancy has increased globally by 21 years since 1950, from 46.6 years to 67.6 years.
• In Japan, women have a life expectancy of 86, the highest in the world.
• Europe has the highest proportion of older people. Older people account for more than 25% of the population in Germany, Italy and Japan.
• In richer regions, one in three of the population will be over 60 by 2050. In poorer regions it will be one in five.

Old age dependency ratio
Japan has the highest ratio, with 34 older persons to every 100 persons of working age, followed closely by Italy and Germany with 31.

How they live
• One out of every seven older persons lives alone.
• About 20% of people aged over 65 are economically active. This is almost the same as in 1980, but labour force participation of men has fallen and that of women has risen.

Pensions
According to the World Bank, only one in four workers will get some sort of pension when they no longer work.
Labor force covered by pension schemes in non-OECD countries:
• East Asia 44% (but China only 20%)
• Middle East and North Africa 34%
• Latin America and the Caribbean 32%
• South Asia 13%
• Sub-Saharan Africa 6%

Median age
This is the age that divides the population in half, with 50 per cent younger and 50 per cent older.
Globally:
• 2009 – median age is 28
• 2050 – median age expected to be 38
The median age in Europe is 40, double that in Africa, where it is 19. ∎

Source: UNPD, World Population Ageing 2009

maximum sagacity – when the rate of brain cells dying is outweighed by the rate of brain cells being created – is reached at the age of 72, he says, emphasizing that older workers have an essential role to play in the workplace.

Housing arrangements are also likely to change. Currently, in the Western world, around five per cent of old people live in nursing or retirement homes. The percentage who do so in the Majority World is tiny by comparison. Many of the world's old people live alone and that number is set to rise as older people become more healthy and more independent.

In the Majority World the challenges presented by population ageing are greater because the process is happening more quickly and the lack of equality and social welfare provision is more acute. Traditionally, people in these countries have relied more upon families than the state to provide a social welfare net. In Latin America and the Middle East, for example, a large proportion of elderly people still live with their families in multigenerational homes.

But this is changing. Globalization and economic migration have broken close family bonds as workers – especially women – seek work abroad to support their families back home. The tendency towards smaller, nuclear families rather than large extended ones has also had an impact on people's willingness to support elderly relatives.

There are reports of older people – again, especially women – being neglected by their families. A shocking news story from Ghana describes how older women are being banished to 'witch camps' by relatives unprepared to care for them or, worse still, being neglected until they die. Journalist Yaw Martin Agyemang Badu reports: 'The cost of caring for these elderly women by their families [is] the root cause for this practice.'[9]

In China, where the one-child policy led to a sharp

drop in births, there is an increased pressure on the younger generation. One daughter or son may have to support six elderly people (parents and grandparents) – and that's before they even start thinking of having a child of their own.

There is also a cultural expectation, more prominent in Asia than in Europe or the Americas, that young and middle-aged people should support their elders. China, though booming economically, has seen a dramatic erosion of social welfare. The authorities are nonetheless worried that large numbers of destitute older people will be neglected by their 'little emperor' offspring.

In early 2011 the Chinese government announced that it was considering making it compulsory for people to visit their aged parents. But many Chinese people of working age now live far from their parents, who may be hundreds of kilometers away in the rural areas.[10] Nor do the authorities acknowledge the part played by government policies – including the dismantling of social welfare – in creating the conditions for old-age poverty and isolation.

The challenge for the world's governments today is to enable citizens to live out their twilight years with dignity. But in China doctors openly discuss 'euthanasia' as a solution, reports journalist Fred

Ushi's day

'Ushi Okushima is the oldest resident in Ogimi, the oldest community in Japan, the country with the oldest population in the world. Aged 105 in 2008, she still dabbed a little French perfume behind her ears and sipped at the local firewater before taking to the village dancefloor to demonstrate traditional Japanese folk dancing. Ushi was born into a country only recently departed from the era of *shogun* warlords. Today she works twice a week at the local store, weighing fruit and veg for customers scarcely younger than herself. And she holds court as the world's media come to Ogimi to discover the secrets of "longevity village". It's not a bad advert for ageing. For the future of the world.' ■
Fred Pearce, from *Peoplequake*, Eden Project Books.

Pearce, raising the grim question: could China's leaders impose euthanasia as they imposed birth policies in the past (see Chapter 2)? Better, surely, that China redirect some of its massive trade earnings towards social provision for its ageing citizens. Universal old-age pensions are essential for the world's ageing people and, where they exist, the benefits are often felt by the entire family.

It is said that these demographic changes will disproportionately affect women. Women are likely to be the majority of old people – and women are also likely to be called upon to be the main carers of elderly relatives. But the successes of feminism over the last few decades suggest that the generation of women entering old age today may be better equipped to fight for their rights than their mothers or their grandmothers were.

Proud to be gray

Many of today's old people, both women and men, are already doing so. The Gray Panthers, started in the US by Maggie Kuhn in 1972, have established themselves as a political force with some clout. In Britain, one of the most successful magazines is *The Oldie*, founded by Richard Ingrams, former editor of the satirical *Private Eye*. In China, meanwhile, demonstrations against corruption or for workers and rights in rust-belt industrial towns are often organized by old people. 'Older workers are not afraid. They see no difference between starving to death and being killed,' says one young protester.[11]

When environmental writer Fred Pearce travels around the Western world giving lectures, he finds that some of his best audiences are not students but 'bolshie grays with the skills to sustain argument that they must have learned on the campuses of the 1960s'. While US writer Theodore Roszak reckons that the fact that there will be more older people around increases the chances of a more caring world: 'The old are not a good audience for the dog-eat-dog social ethic. If anything, they create an ambience which favors the survival of the gentlest.'[11]

Perhaps the graying of nations is not in itself a crisis. Poverty is, inequality is, and so is the failure to raise taxes and redistribute wealth more evenly through social welfare. Rather than lamenting the ageing of populations, our attention might be better directed towards building a more sustainable economic system that enables ordinary people to work and also to be able, at some point, to stop working.

World population is ageing, predictably, over time. Adapting to it will require some planning, but also a more open-minded and innovative approach to all the areas of human life and activity that the UN warns will be affected by population ageing. Work, health, housing, pensions, education – the lot.

1 United Nations Population Division (UNPD), *World Population Ageing 2009*, New York 2009. **2** UNICEF, 'Levels and Trends in Child Mortality', 16 Sep 2010. **3** Fred Pearce, 'The Population Crash', The Guardian, 1 Feb 2010. **4** Roberto Ham-Chande et al, *Ageing in Developing Countries: Building Bridges for Integrated Research Agendas*, IUSSP Policy and Research Papers, 2009. **5** UNPD, *World Population Prospects: the 2008 Revision*, 2009. **6** Jill Curnow, 'Myths and the Fear of an Ageing Population', AESP Occasional Paper, Oct 2000. **7** Robert Kunzig, 'Population 7 billion', *National Geographic*, Jan 2011. **8** Sarah Sexton, 'Too Many Grannies? The politics of Population Aging', *Different Takes*, The Publication of the Population and Development Program at Hampshire College, No 42, Fall 2006. **9** Yaw Martin Agyemang Badu, 'Ageing in Dignity', Ghana Web, 29 Dec 2010. **10** BBC World Service, 6 Jan 2011. **11** Fred Pearce, *Peoplequake*, Eden Project Books, 2010.

4 A woman's body

The idea that women should have control over their own bodies and their own fertility is not new. But prudes, priests and patriarchs are fighting it tooth and nail. The impact is being felt most keenly in sub-Saharan Africa, where family planning is cast as an attack on African fertility – with fatal consequences.

'WE SHOULD BE talking about sex!' said one family-planning promoter. She was exasperated at how arcane and mathematical discussions of population can get.

'Population is sex action!' she insisted. 'It's about man and woman having sex!'

Or not having it – as the Bush administration, the Vatican and other 'abstinence' ideologues prefer.

One of the first things President Obama did on coming to office was indicate that he would reverse the 'global gag rule' which for seven years had blocked $244 million of US funding for family planning around the world.

Heavily influenced by the Christian Right, the Bush administration had prohibited overseas organizations from receiving US family-planning assistance if they used their non-US funds to provide abortion information, services or counseling, or engaged in any abortion-rights advocacy.

Furthermore, money was directed away from pro-condom campaigns and into 'abstinence-only' drives.

The condom stopped being the ideal item to help protect against both HIV and unwanted pregnancy, and was vilified instead. The latex demon 'encouraged promiscuity' and, its detractors argued with a logic of medieval perversity, thereby *caused* the spread of HIV. Typical of anti-condom propaganda is a Tanzanian poster, displayed near a school in March

2008, depicting a skeleton and captioned: 'Faithful condom user'.

Such campaigns were especially effective in sub-Saharan Africa – a region with the world's highest fertility rates, lowest contraceptive use and highest

Every sperm is sacred...

Religious hostility to family planning has a long and bitter history.

Many and colorful have been the condemnations of the evils of contraception coming from the Vatican over the centuries. The theological bases for the repeated objections have been obscure to say the least. But the propaganda has been at times simple, crude and telling.

A successful 1948 campaign ad in the Massachusetts *Catholic Mirror* shows a baby lying asleep in a cot. Across the baby's blanket are written the words: 'Tomorrow's children'. Above the child, an arm is wielding a knife that is about to be punched into the baby's neck. On the knife blade is written: 'birth control'; on the arm: 'planned parenthood'.

In 1981 Catholic priest Paul Marx set up Human Life International (HLI) to campaign against contraception and abortion. He urged US bishops to act against the IUD and the Pill, which were 'killing millions of future Catholics'. By 1987 HLI had gained Vatican funding and expanded to 18 branches abroad, shipping propaganda to over 100 countries.

In more recent times, Catholic anxiety about numbers has resurfaced as evangelical Protestant churches have become more popular. Both strands of Christianity are concerned about the comparative increase of Muslims in the world.

Though Islam is more open to family planning – at the 1994 Cairo conference Pakistan's Benazir Bhutto held a torch for women's reproductive rights – some of the more patriarchal elements are finding agreement with their Christian rivals. They too want to increase numbers and to limit women's autonomy.

In reality, many women around the world are managing to ignore the male priesthood when it comes to their own bodies. In Catholic-majority Latin America, for example, contraceptive uptake is 70 per cent or more. The current Pope can look even closer to home for an example of how much notice women take of the Vatican position: Italian women have one of the lowest fertility rates in western Europe. No-one is suggesting it's because they have stopped having sex with men. ∎

Sources: Matthew Connelly, *Fatal Misconception*, Kelknap Harvard, 2008, and Fred Pearce, *Peoplequake*, Eden Project Books, 2010.

incidence of unsafe abortion. It is also the region most devastated by AIDS. Anti-condom propaganda popped up everywhere. I recall a Kenyan health professional telling me that condoms were useless because they had 'lots of tiny holes in them'.

The damage done is probably immeasurable. But it was made easier by not-so-distant memories of coercive and deceitful 'population control' drives that have targeted people in developing countries. These give resonance to current religious claims that contraception is all about trying to stop Africans having babies; that family planning is, in short, an assault on African fertility and African culture.

Uganda, which during the 1990s had a bold, proactive and effective HIV prevention policy based on widespread promotion of condoms, had by 2005 turned anti-condom and pro-abstinence. 'Abstinence' parties and rallies were held for youth. Without much success. Although nine out of ten young Ugandans surveyed rate religion as an 'important' part of their lives, half of 15-19 year olds have had sex. The country has one of the highest fertility rates in the region.

'We don't think abstinence is really working in our communities,' concludes a youth leader from Kabarole. 'We always come with the message to delay sexual début. But for most [school students] here, this is not enough.'[1]

People go on having sex, without protection, with consequences.

Abortion capital

Worldwide, the abortion rate is declining. But not in sub-Saharan Africa, where it is mainly illegal and unsafe. The country with the highest unsafe abortion rate in the world is Nigeria, where one in ten women of childbearing age have had one.[2] According to conservative estimates, unsafe abortion claims the lives of more than 3,000 women a year here, which is why Nigeria's maternal mortality rate – 840 deaths per 100,000 live births – is one of the world's highest.[3]

Women die of complications caused by incomplete abortion, infection and excessive blood loss. Or they may suffer septic shock and trauma to reproductive and other organs. One in four Nigerian women who have abortions experience serious complications but only one third of these seek the emergency medical treatment they need.

Poor women are most at risk from unsafe abortions because they rely on traditional methods; richer women tend to use the services of health professionals operating clandestinely.

Often deaths are hushed up. Asked whether death from abortion was common in her community, a 20-year-old Nigerian student responded: 'Maybe it happens, but who will tell you somebody died from abortion? If someone dies, they will say it is from a brief illness.'[4]

Abortion is most common among women who are young, unmarried and childless. Women like Grace, a student living in a Nigerian city. She first had sex when she was 15, but never used contraception because she didn't believe she would get pregnant. It was also against her religious beliefs and she feared side-effects. She became pregnant at 18 and decided to

---

Falling and rising

Worldwide the number of abortions fell from an estimated 45.5 million procedures in 1995 to 41.6 million in 2003. But in Africa they rose from 5.0 million to 5.6 million, only 100,000 of which were performed under safe conditions.

An estimated 92% of women of childbearing age in Africa live in countries with restrictive abortion laws. It is absolutely forbidden in 14.

The World Health Organization estimates that in Africa one in seven maternal deaths results from unsafe abortion. ■

Source: Guttmacher Institute, Abortion Worldwide: A Decade of Uneven Progress, 2009.

have an abortion because she did not want to drop out of school. She was also afraid of the shame it would cause her parents and the man who had made her pregnant if she carried the baby to term.[2]

In Nigeria the proportion of women who have unsafe abortions is higher among Catholics (19 per cent) than among Protestants and Muslims (11 per cent and 5 per cent respectively) – even though Catholicism is the religion most damning of abortion. When women are desperate, legal or religious sanctions have little impact. In western Europe, where abortion is legal, the rate is 12 per 1,000. In Africa where it is mainly illegal, it is 29 – and even this figure is probably too low due to under-reporting.[5]

When the gate is barred
In 1987 Betsy Hartmann wrote: 'We call on the world to recognize women's basic right to control their own bodies and to have access to the power, resources and reproductive health services that ensure that they can do so.'

In many parts of the world women are still denied those basic rights. The abortion rate in sub-Saharan Africa is high for the same reasons that fertility is high: family planning is not reaching women who need it and religio-political hostility to contraception prevails.

A high rate of risky abortion is the clearest of all indications that there is a serious unmet need for contraception. In the world generally, poor and rural women are least likely to get the contraception they need. But in sub-Saharan Africa all women find it difficult. For single and unmarried women, getting hold of contraceptives is especially tricky. Researcher Agnès Guillaume explains: 'Family planning is often delivered only through mother-and-child clinics. This is no good for unmarried women without children.'

Poverty and sexism increase the risk of unwanted

pregnancy, especially for the young. Young women and girls who are poor may trade sex for money. More than half of adolescents surveyed in Malawi had experienced forced sex and 60 per cent had accepted money or gifts in exchange for sex. And although 90 per cent of 15-19 year olds approved of contraception, most who were sexually active did not use it.[6]

For married women, gender inequality can play out in different ways. Sometimes women are stopped from using contraception by husbands who fear that it will encourage them to 'play around'. But one of the most common reasons given by both women and men for not using methods of contraception other than condoms (such as the Pill, the IUD, injectables and emergency contraception) is anxiety about unwanted effects – especially infertility.

Abortion is perceived as safer than contraception. A 22-year-old Nigerian undergraduate commented: 'One D and C [early abortion] is safer than 16 packs of daily pills... many girls say this.'[4]

When asked what forms of contraception they were familiar with, young Nigerians mentioned alum, potash, snuff, white quinine, brandy, Krest (a non-alcoholic mineral drink), detergent, lime water and various hormonal preparations. Several

---

Missing girls

Sex-selective abortion is illegal in India, yet it is committed an estimated one million times a year.

Various ways are found around the illegality. Codes may be used when ultrasounds are done to tell parents the gender of the child – for example: 'If the doctor tells us to come and get an ultrasound report on a Monday we know it's a boy. Friday means a girl.'

In China, sex-selective abortion following an ultrasound scan is legal and has, in many cases, replaced female infanticide. In 2006 China had 83 girls for every 100 boys. China's 'missing girls' count over the past 30 years is now estimated to be 25 to 30 million. ∎

Source: Fred Pearce, *Peoplequake*, Eden Project Books, 2010.

students believed that antibiotics and aspirin worked as contraceptives. Many did not even mention the condom as a contraceptive method, as they thought of it more as a means of preventing infections than of avoiding pregnancy.

Such lack of knowledge is not restricted to adolescents. It is common for married women with unwanted pregnancies to say they did not use contraception because they didn't have sex very often.

What's needed?

Campaigners have their list. Accurate information, widely disseminated, for a start. A full range of contraceptive services with a broad range of methods to suit different people in different circumstances. Guidance, counseling, training on family planning in universities, hospitals, schools. Reform of laws that restrict access to abortion. Better abortion and post-abortion care. Comprehensive, affordable, quality health services publicly provided.

And, last but not least, talking. As the exasperated delegate said, population is 'sex action'. That means setting prudish taboos aside and discussing contraception and the wide range of non-procreative sex options that exist. It means being realistic about sex – and acknowledging the unreality of abstinence.

A word of caution, though. Women have too often been seen as the cause of the 'population problem' – and are still regarded in this light today. In a much-viewed YouTube video, US comedian Doug Stanhope says to the world's women: 'Your combined uteri wreak more havoc to the environment than 1,000 Dow Chemical accidents combined...'

There is, in some quarters, a near hysterical level of concern about sub-Saharan Africa's high fertility rate, which is cited as an indication of a 'population time-bomb'. This view is not shared by the *Economist* magazine, which believes that the region probably

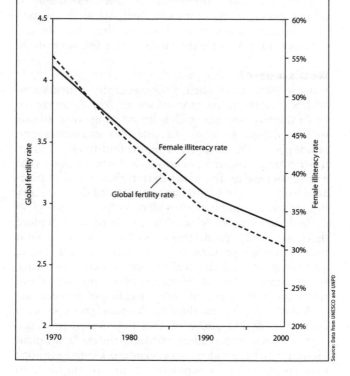

Global decline in female illiteracy and fertility

The lines speak for themselves – if a girl or woman is literate, she is far more likely to have control over her own fertility and to have greater choice in the number of children she bears.

needs population growth in order to fuel its next stage of development.

Certainly, the fertility rate – at an average five children per woman – is high compared with other parts of the world. But life expectancy is also shockingly low – around 50 years in 17 sub-Saharan countries. The tragedy of AIDS accounts for this in part, but more significant still is simple and persistent poverty.

The family-planning industry, starved of funds during the Bush years, is not beyond tapping Western anxiety about 'too many African babies' in order to get the lines of funding restored. Some, like the influential Population Action International, have deployed fears of overpopulation to win broader support inside and outside Congress.

There are excellent human rights reasons for responding to women's need for access to a range of high-quality contraceptive choices. That is enough in itself – without bothering about human numbers. In fact, it is better if numbers and targets are kept out of it.

As Betsy Hartmann comments: 'There's a long and sordid history of population control programs violating women's rights and harming their health. That's why feminist reformers in the international family-planning field have fought hard to make programs responsive to women's – and men's – real reproductive and sexual health needs... A world of difference exists between services that treat women as population targets, and those based on a feminist model of respectful, holistic, high-quality care.'[7]

Her earlier observation still holds true: 'The great irony is that in most cases population growth comes down faster the less you focus on it as a policy priority and the more you focus on women's rights and basic human human needs.'

The evidence is everywhere. From Bangladesh to Brazil, programs that focused on women's empowerment – including education – in the past two decades have had dramatic and lasting effects. Bangladesh's women are having half the number of children their mothers had. In Brazil, too, family size has halved in the past 25 years to an average of 2.2 children.

A woman's right to control her own body and to have access to the power, resources and reproductive health services to ensure she can do so: these things are key. Keep the focus on improving women's health, women's education, women's rights – and the rest can take care of itself.

1 Human Rights Watch, 'The less they know, the better', Washington, 2005 www.hrw.org 2 Guttmacher Institute, 'Unwanted Pregnancy and Induced Abortion in Nigeria', New York, 2006. 3 UNICEF, *The State of the World's Children 2011.* 4 V Otoide, F Oronsaye, F Okonofua,'Why Nigerian Adolescents Seek Abortion rather than Contraception: Evidence from Focus Group Discussion', *International Family Planning Perspectives*, 2001. 5 Guttmacher Institute, 'Facts on Induced Abortion worldwide', 2008. 6 Guttmacher Institute, 'Adolescence in Malawi: Sexual and Reproductive Health', 2005. 7 Betsy Hartmann, 'The "New" Population Control Craze: Retro, Racist, Wrong Way to Go', *On The Issues Magazine*, 2005.

5 For richer, for poorer

Get rid of poverty! Stop poor people breeding! The crude mantra has new followers today – and novel permutations. And for the rich... order your designer babies now.

IT SOUNDED GOOD. 'I want poor families to have the same access to family planning as rich families,' Peruvian President Alberto Fujimori told his people.

What followed, however, was far from generous or equitable. Operating from the premise that you could fight poverty by reducing the birth rate, President Fujimori's government launched an ambitious-sounding family-planning program to great fanfare and acclaim at the 1995 UN Conference on Women at Beijing. Backing came from the World Bank, the renamed United Nations Population Fund (UNFPA) and USAID.

But it was a program of fear and coercion that prioritized surgical sterilization, targeted the wombs of poor women and moved with alarming rapidity. In the first seven months, 64,841 women underwent tubal ligations. By 2000, more than 300,000 women and 30,000 men had been sterilized. In many cases women were lied to or forced to undergo the operation against their wishes. Many of the women were illiterate Quechua speakers, who did not know what they were letting themselves in for.

With more candor than his political bosses had shown, one member of a sterilizing team told documentary filmmaker Mathilde Damoisel that the health workers believed that the best way to tackle poverty was to tackle the poor.[1] A quota system was created. Health units were encouraged to compete with each other and incentives were offered to those who found women to sterilize.

'After my son was born,' says one victim, 'they

asked me: "do you want to breed like a rabbit, live like a sow?". They told me I had to get my tubes tied. They didn't listen to me.'

Officially 17 women died, though many more were left with permanent physical and psychological damage as a result of their ordeals.

'I feel like half my body is dead. I tell my children I am dead. Like my other friends who are already dying. All the mothers I know who have been sterilized feel like this,' said one woman.

It took a while for the scandal to make it to Peru's national media. Once it had, the UNFPA and USAID said they could not support a program that used coercion. The quotas were dropped after 1997 but the program was not abandoned.

Peruvian vice-health minister Alejandro Aguinaga was unrepentant. The reduction in the birth rate from 3.4 to 2.2 had brought Peru 'into the modern world,' he told Damoisel.[1]

It is true that as people become richer they tend to have fewer children. But it does not follow that poverty can be reduced by lowering the birth rate of poor people. Trying to do so quickly turns into a war on poor people. Peru's policy-makers, and the international funders that backed them, need only have looked at what happened 20 years earlier in India to see that Peru's target-driven program was likely to be a human rights disaster.

During the 1970s India launched population-control measures which one leading official proudly described as 'a frontal assault on the citadels of poverty'. It turned out to be more than a metaphor, as forced sterilizations were accompanied by a slum clearance program. In Delhi alone, 700,000 people were driven from their homes.

Many lost their lives while resisting the slum clearances and as a result of the forced sterilizations. One victim was an 80-year-old man who had been

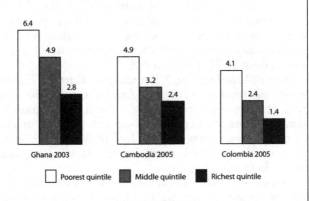

Total fertility rate by wealth

Average number of children born to a woman during her lifetime

Ghana 2003: 6.4, 4.9, 2.8
Cambodia 2005: 4.9, 3.2, 2.4
Colombia 2005: 4.1, 2.4, 1.4

☐ Poorest quintile ◼ Middle quintile ◼ Richest quintile

Poorer women tend to have more children than richer ones because, denied educational possibilities, they will start having chidren younger. Lack of equality in healthcare and nutrition increases the risk of child mortality, creating an incentive for poor women to have more children.

Source: 2007 Population Reference Bureau

forcibly vasectomized. Again, there were quotas to fill.[2]

'Should never have been born at all'

'Stop poor people breeding' has been the mantra of the privileged for some time. In certain states in mid-19th century Germany, poor men aged under 30 were not allowed to marry.

Population-control pioneer Margaret Sanger captured middle-class frustration with, fear of, and hostility towards poor people when in 1922 she wrote: 'We are paying for, even submitting to the dictates of an ever-increasing class of human beings who should never have been born at all.'

She went on: 'Every feeble-minded girl or woman of a hereditary type, especially of the moron class, should be segregated during her reproductive period.'[3]

C Lalor Burdick, a major donor to the Planned Parenthood Federation of America in the 1960s, put it bluntly when he said that welfare programs were 'breeding pads and free sustenance for the proliferation of the kind of people that hate us and would destroy us if they could'.[2]

In 1974 influential US biologist Garrett Hardin wrote an article entitled 'Lifeboat ethics: the case against helping the poor'. He argued that 'a nation's land has a limited capacity to support population and, as the current energy crisis has shown us, in some ways we have already exceeded the carrying capacity of our land'.[4]

Hardin was echoing the Malthusian view that there was no point in helping the poor because it would only encourage them to breed – and breeding was the reason they were poor. For several decades Western governments and international institutions reflected such thinking in their policies towards Majority World countries suffering from debt. Foreign aid and loans were used to coercive – and sometimes violent – effect.

When Kenya needed a structural adjustment loan, the World Bank agreed on condition that the country accepted a program to reduce fertility. Kenya's ministry of health initially objected, but the cash-starved government did what so many poor women have done under similar pressure – it caved in.

Bangladesh was even more bound to the wishes of richer nations. By the early 1980s, Western 'population assistance' accounted for two-thirds of the country's national budget. Eager to keep the aid money flowing, soldiers were ordered to round up poor people for forced sterilizations in 1983. During disastrous floods in 1984, in four districts food aid was denied to those who did not agree to sterilization. Even children and the elderly were sterilized. The 'motivators' had their quotas to fill.

And the richer...

C Lalor Burdick, the wealthy US donor to the Planned Parenthood Federation of America quoted above, had another complaint. He said it was a mistake of family planners to proceed with plans for a two-child family as a universal standard. 'Would it not be better if the truly useful families should have three or four children and those who have demonstrated themselves as feckless should not have any?'[2]

That is the other side of the 'poor should not breed' coin: the rich should breed more. In 1983 Singapore introduced a policy designed to achieve both aims. Poor women of the Malay minority were offered $5,000 if they agreed to be sterilized; meanwhile graduates were offered tax breaks if they bore three or four children.

There are signs that affluent couples in the US and Britain are tending to go for a larger family size again. Such income-rich families may hire nannies from, for example, the Philippines. Frequently mothers themselves, these nannies will have had to leave their own children behind – a theme explored in director Lukas Moodyson's film *Mammoth*. In an era of globalization, the right to know your own children as they grow up is also determined by wealth – or lack of it.

Not only are rich people encouraged to have children, they also are getting to choose their babies. First, there's the gender. Journalist Carla Power found that sex selection in India was especially prevalent among the wealthier, urban middle classes and élites. Male fetuses went full-term, females were aborted.

'India's female [sex-selective abortion] problem is

entwined with the consumer society. If one can order a BMW, goes the mindset, one can order a boy,' writes Power.[5]

Namita Sharma of the University of Jammu adds: 'Educated women are more efficient at discriminating against daughters.'[5]

British journalist Fred Pearce was told: 'If you go to Delhi, ask around the World Bank offices about how many of the staff there have had daughters and you will be very surprised. There are virtually none.'

In a study of middle-class couples in the northern state of Punjab, 73 per cent of women said that if a sex test showed the fetus to be female it should be aborted. Sex selection may be illegal in India, but clinics in Mumbai are making a fortune offering scans and abortions. Doctors can get a fee of $870 for carrying out a sex test followed by abortion.[5]

Other advances in medical technology have not only privileged rich prospective parents but also given birth to a booming 'baby business'. For example, in-vitro fertilization is increasingly in demand but there is only limited availability within the public health system. Mostly it is available only to those who can afford it. Meanwhile the commercial trade in eggs, sperm and even embryos has become a multi-billion-dollar global business. In early 2011 the assisted-reproduction industry in the US was reported to be worth $3 billion and, unlike that in Canada or Britain, is largely unregulated.[6]

In the US, 'egg hunters' act as internet brokers between recipient and donors. One donor told the *New York Daily News* that she sold her eggs to pay the rent.[7] A classified ad on the online *Daily Bruin* student newsletter of UCLA read: 'We are seeking women who have blue-green eyes, are under the age of 29, SAT 1300+, physically fit... $20,000 (plus expenses).'

Jesse Reynolds of the Center for Genetics and

Society public advocacy group in Oakland expressed concern: 'Self-regulation from these companies is inadequate. The types of dangers that come to mind when certain traits of donors are being sought include the notion of breeding better humans.'[7]

Bespoke babies

The dangers that Reynolds referred to are already happening. In San Antonio US entrepreneur Jennalee Ryan has set up Abraham Center of Life, which enables childless clients to custom-make an embryo. Ryan buys sperm from labs that require donors to have doctorate degrees. She hires only attractive egg donors in their twenties with college educations. She then sends both the sperm and eggs to a doctor who creates the embryos.[8]

Another growth area is surrogacy, whereby a woman agrees to carry and have a baby for a childless couple. In the past this was often done in the spirit of helping out friends or relatives who were unable to bear a child themselves, but increasingly it is being done on a commercial basis. Typically, a poorer woman will 'rent her womb' to a richer childless couple for several thousand dollars.

As with so many services in the global economy, it is now far cheaper to 'outsource' surrogacy to poorer regions. It is also likely to be less tightly regulated. India is fast becoming the surrogacy hub of choice for Westerners.[9] Clinics that provide surrogate mothers for foreigners say they have been inundated with requests from the US and Europe as word spreads of India's combination of skilled medical professionals, relatively liberal laws and low prices.

Commercial surrogacy, which is banned in some European countries and subject to regulation in US states, is legally a gray area in India. The cost of the medical procedures, air tickets and hotels for two trips to India (one for the fertilization and a second to collect the baby) comes to around $25,000, roughly a third of the typical price in the US.

Of that, $7,500 may go to the surrogate mother. Immediately she has given birth, the baby will be handed to the future parents who, in most cases, the birth-mother will not meet. Under guidelines issued by the Indian Medical Council, surrogate mothers sign away all their rights to the child. In cases where the surrogate provides a womb for an embryo formed from the sperm and egg of the prospective parents, it is only the names of these genetic parents that appear on the birth certificate. If an egg donor is involved, her

Moral dilemmas and urgent questions

By allowing the fertility industry to experiment with new techniques and protocols with little oversight, and by uncritically embracing these new technologies, we have put women and children at risk.

We believe that it is time for our community to undertake a pro-active, in-depth, critical analysis of the safety concerns and ethical dilemmas posed by new reproductive and genetic technologies. Here we suggest some of the key ethical questions to be addressed:

• Is there an essential difference between a woman's right to terminate an unwanted pregnancy and the decision to pre-select the traits of her children?

• What will be the effects of trait de-selection on people living with disabilities and on society in general?

• Should fertility clinics be permitted to market procedures that allow the selection of future children's eye, hair and skin color, as one did in 2009?

• Is it politically acceptable to condemn sex selection in countries where it is used to avoid girl children, yet accept a burgeoning and lucrative sex selection business in the US and Canada for 'family balancing'?

• Do payments to poor women in India for surrogacy services or to young women for eggs benefit these women more than exploit them? How do we create an ethical framework that accounts both for people's desire to have a biologically related child and concerns about risks to egg donors or surrogates?

• Do selection and de-selection technologies serve as a gateway to extreme procedures such as reproductive cloning and inheritable genetic modification? ■

From: Marcy Darnovsky, Francine Coeytaux, and Susan Berke Fogel, 'Assisted reproduction and choice in the biotech age: recommendations for a way forward', Center for Genetics and Society, Oakland, US, 1 Jan 2011.

name does not appear on the document, either; only that of the father.

Amelia Gentleman, reporting on one case for the *New York Times*, writes: 'In the clinic, it is clear that an exchange between rich and poor is under way. On some of the contracts, the thumbprint of an illiterate surrogate stands out against the signatures of the clients.'

Dr Kausal Kadam who works at the Rotunda clinic in Mumbai says: 'Surrogates do it to give their children better education, to buy a home, to start up a small business, a shop. This is as much money as they could earn in maybe three years. I really don't think that this is exploiting the women. I feel it is two people who are helping out each other.'

Some people in India are calling for regulation of the commercial surrogacy industry. But *The Times of India* questions how such a law would be enforced: 'In a country crippled by abject poverty, how will the government body guarantee that women will not agree to surrogacy just to be able to eat two square meals a day?'

For many Western would-be parents, the price is what attracts them to India. Lisa Switzer, a Texan medical technician in her forties, comments: 'Doctors, lawyers, accountants, they can afford it, but the rest of us – the teachers, the nurses, the secretaries – we can't. Unless we go to India.'[9]

Reproductive equality
In themselves, new reproductive technologies that enable infertile people to have children are a wonder. But the privatization of population control through their use has profound social ramifications. Ultrasound sex tests are already perpetuating patriarchy in the world's most populous countries, India and China.

In the West, parents are increasingly offered – in the interests of fetal health – 'genetic counseling'. As

For richer, for poorer

Matthew Connelly observes: 'In everyday conversation, people ascribe a whole range of behaviors to good or bad genes, faithfully reciting a eugenic catechism without the faintest idea where it comes from or where it can lead.'

We need, Connelly argues, a new agenda that can renew and revive the cause of reproductive freedom. That should include working together to ensure that everyone – rich and poor – has access both to family planning and to childcare without being coerced to have more or fewer children. Infertility treatment should be available to all equally – not just the privileged few who can afford it. Otherwise we are just repeating the classist and eugenic pronouncements, albeit in different language, about who should and who should not be born.

And it's worth re-examining those commonly expressed fears of 'overcrowding'. Often they have a psychology rooted in the gap between rich and poor. Rarely does a full opera house provoke the complaint that the world is overpopulated. Crowded inner city areas and slums do. In part that's because a lot of poor people have to share a small area. But it is also because when the 'haves' are faced with the prospects of large numbers of 'have-nots' they feel uneasy.

Many people are drawn to cities *because* of their population density. Others, in search of work, have little choice. Those densely populated poor areas of the world's biggest cities are often insanitary.

But Almas Ali of the Population Foundation in India told Robert Kunzig recently that the goal in India should not be reducing fertility or population. The goal should be to make the villages more viable. 'Whenever we talk of population in India, even today, what comes to our mind is the increasing numbers. And the numbers are looked at with fright. This phobia has penetrated the mind-set so much that all the focus is on reducing the number. The focus on people has been pushed to the background.'[10]

There is another issue which has a bearing on wealth, poverty and population size. While the rich consume so much more of the world's resources per head than the poor, the argument for limiting family size should surely apply to the rich first, if it applies at all.

The 'problem' with global population – if there is one – is too many rich people consuming too much, not too many poor people.

But, more of that later...

1 Mathilde Damoisel, *A Woman's Womb*, Tancrede Ramonet, 2010. 2 Matthew Connelly, *Fatal Misconception*, Belknap Harvard, 2008. 3 Robert Engelman, *More*, Island Press, 2008. 4 Garrett Hardin, 'Lifeboat ethics: the case against helping the poor', *Psychology Today*, 1974. 5 Fred Pearce, *Peoplequake*, Eden Project Books, 2010. 6 Genetics and Society, Oakland, US, 2011. 7 Evan Pondel, 'A Booming Baby Business', *New York Daily News*, Apr 2006. 8 Juju Chang and Deborah Apton, 'Woman Says She Runs The World's First Donor-Created Human Embryo Bank', *ABC News*, 22 Feb 2007. 9 Amelia Gentleman, 'Foreign couples turn to India for surrogate mothers', *New York Times*, 4 Mar 2008. 10 Robert Kunzig, 'Population 7 billion', *National Geographic*, Jan 2011.

6 On the move

The flow of migrants around the world is the hardest thing for demographers to predict. It is also the subject of the most fierce – and often ill-informed – political debate.

'SEVENTY MILLION IS too many,' read the headline. A number of British parliamentarians, including the former Archbishop of Canterbury, Dr George Carey, had issued a 'declaration on population'.

They were responding to an Office of National Statistics projection that Britain's population, currently just over 60 million, could reach 70 million by 2029 if current trends continued. With Britons barely reproducing themselves, most of the population growth would come as a result of immigration. This, the parliamentarians' declaration said, would have 'a significant impact on our public services, our quality of life and the nature of our society'.[1]

In an interview on BBC radio, Dr Carey insisted that he was concerned about the numbers, not about the type of people who were coming into the country. But as the discussion proceeded it became clear that 'the type' mattered – a lot. The people admitted would be those who would fit in with the 'Christian traditions' of the country, said Lord Carey. Furthermore, he advocated a 'values-based' immigration policy that might produce a higher proportion of Christian immigrants. The interviewer was too polite to mention the fact that fewer than half the British population surveyed claim to 'believe in God'.[2]

The point of the 'population declaration' put forward by Carey and others was to get party leaders to commit to reduce net annual immigration to below 40,000, returning to levels last seen in the early 1990s.

Politicians from both the major parties fell over themselves to assure the British public that their population would not be allowed to reach 70 million. Conservative David Cameron announced that immigration would have to be cut by 75 per cent to achieve this.

This precisely mirrors the demands of the anti-immigration pressure group Migration Watch, which states: 'To keep the population of the UK below 70 million, immigration must be reduced by 75 per cent.'[3]

Big Australia vs little Australia

In Australia, too, concerns about population and immigration are bundled together. The result is no less controversial. A report from the federal Treasury foresaw Australia's population growing by almost two-thirds over the next 40 years to 36 million – about 25 per cent higher than the Treasury had predicted just three years earlier. Some of the boom would be home-grown, as young Australian women are having more children than did their baby-boomer predecessors. But a larger proportion will come from immigration.[4]

Up to 2009, Australia had been taking about 244,000 immigrants a year. The then-Prime minister Kevin Rudd had remarked: 'I actually believe in a big Australia – I make no apology for that. I actually think it's good news that our population is growing.'

Rudd's comment kicked off a storm of protest. It became a flashpoint on talkback radio shows and reflected badly in polls. One man, PR executive William Bourke, was so incensed he started the Stable Population Party of Australia, dedicated to cutting immigration and pegging Australian population at its current 23 million.

MP Kelvin Thomson, of Rudd's own Australian Labor Party, cited a long list of global issues, from traffic congestion and waste, to global warming and terrorism, and explained how the population explosion was at the base of each of these problems. Other like-minded public figures included the former New South

Wales premier Bob Carr, singer John Williamson and Clean Up Australia founder Ian Kiernan.

The furore had its desired political impact. A big national debate was conducted via mass and social media and, in her first announcement after taking office, Rudd's successor Julia Gillard rejected the 'big Australia' policy, telling voters she did not believe in it. 'Australia should not hurtle down the track towards a big population,' she said.[5]

But the country's leading demographer Peter McDonald and two other government advisers were quick to warn Gillard to reject 'little Australia'. The nation's 'big Australia' debate had now entered 'dangerous territory', they said, as they pressed the case for higher immigration to keep the economy strong.

'Migrants are being used as a scapegoat for the failures of government planning,' said McDonald, head of the Australian Demographic and Social Research Institute. 'You don't want to go down the track of bringing out the worst in Australians.'

Business leaders also warned of the risks of any move to use population pressures as a reason to scale back on immigration numbers, saying they were crucial to future economic growth.[6]

The perception that Australia is the destination point of choice for many of the world's refugees is exaggerated by repeated TV footage of 'boat people'. Writing in *The Age*, Ross Gittins comments: 'Some people imagine the boat people explain the high levels of migration in recent years, but that's quite wrong. Their numbers are trivial in the scheme of things, and don't increase the modest total of refugees admitted each year.' Using Productivity Commission figures, he concluded that, in spite of all the fuss, migration would slow down in the next few years.[7]

Meanwhile, in the United States, the Federation for American Immigration Reform (FAIR) maintains that it's only immigration that is keeping the

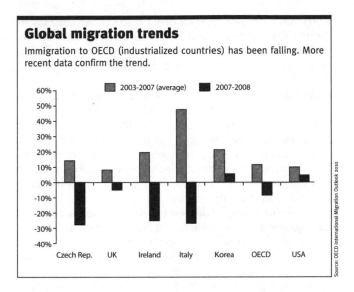

Global migration trends

Immigration to OECD (industrialized countries) has been falling. More recent data confirm the trend.

2003-2007 (average) ■ 2007-2008

Source: OECD International Migration Outlook 2010

nation's fertility rate up and that immigration-driven population growth is to blame for the huge increase in US CO_2 emissions from between 1973 and 2007. Immigration, its website says, is 'straining our environment and quality of life'. US anti-immigrant groups, many of which have their roots in supremacist and eugenic organizations, blame immigration for everything from urban sprawl to crime, from traffic congestion to terrorism. Even the sub-prime crisis has been attributed to immigrants.[8]

Even in Canada, a country that has traditionally been the most welcoming to immigrants, Immigration Watch Canada is gaining support for the view that the current levels are unsustainable.

Reality check

Judging by all the heat, you would think that the rate of immigration into richer countries must be escalating. In fact it has been slowing down for several years now, having peaked around 2007. At the end of 2010 there were around 214 million migrants in the world. Of those, 60 per cent were living in so-called 'developed' countries. It's a majority – but not an overwhelming one.[9]

What's keeping the numbers of migrants high is not economic migration, which was declining even before the recession began, but the large number of refugees who are fleeing conflict-torn parts of the world, such as Iraq, Afghanistan and Somalia. And the countries that have seen the biggest increase in refugees arriving at their borders are neighboring countries in Asia or Africa.

Since the global financial crisis, attitudes towards immigration have soured in receiving countries – especially in the richer countries where fears of scarcity are inflamed by racist politicians. There has been some voluntary state repatriation of economic migrants – for example of Ecuadorians from Spain – but no evidence of large-scale return. For many migrants, the better option is to hang on in there,

---

Keeping the family

Remittances – the money migrants send home – have dropped for the first time since 1980 due to the global financial crisis. They declined from $336 billion in 2008 to an estimated $316 billion in 2009. This is especially serious for families in countries reliant on such income. In many of these countries, the imposition of free trade has flooded their markets with foreign imports and destroyed local industry and employment.

Remittances from family members working abroad get directly back to the people – unlike much government-to-government aid. Money from relatives can help families build a home, start a business and so on. And as direct foreign investment has slumped due to the global recession, remittances have become proportionally more significant as a source of income for developing countries. ∎

Sources: UN Statement of the Global Migration group, Athens 4-5 Nov 2009 and Statement of Hania Zlotnik, director of UN Population Division, New York 27 Oct 2010.

---

take lower-paid or informal work if necessary, or get temporary support from families back home until the situation improves.[10]

Illegal immigration, on which the US economy has long depended to fill gaps in its labor market, fell by seven per cent in 2009 to 10.8 million, coinciding with the country's financial crisis, according to the Department of Homeland Security. The majority of the country's illegal immigrants come from Latin America. 'The number of unauthorized residents declined by 1.0 million between 2007 and 2009, coincident with the US economic downturn,' said the report, based on census data and extrapolations from the total foreign population in the country. [11]

Racism, restriction and risk

Many Western governments have responded to the economic crisis by tightening up on immigration. They have been adopting more restrictive requirements for obtaining entry which has made it more irregular and risky for migrants, especially the most vulnerable – unaccompanied children, for example. Restrictions reinforce the impression that migration is a questionable, criminal phenomenon, thereby contributing to anti-immigrant, xenophobic reactions in destination countries.

Bob Hughes of the No One is Illegal group sees in today's burgeoning population politics a resurgence of forms of racism that seemed to have been 'banished into the moral wilderness in the early 1990s'. He comments: 'Identifying yet more scapegoats and subjecting them to yet more controls will absolutely not help us through our economic and ecological crisis. On the contrary, it is these very attitudes to, and abuse of, human beings and their rights, which immigration controls exemplify so perfectly, that brought this crisis about.'[12]

At times of recession the human rights of migrants

are especially vulnerable and so must be defended with renewed vigilance, says the UN's Global Migration Group. Assistant Secretary General Carlos Lopes says: 'Human mobility is a fundamental component of human freedom. States must be vigilant against xenophobic sentiments and discriminatory practices prompted by the economic crisis.'

Female migrants, he said, must be adequately

Migrants and locals clash in Italy

Angry migrants, mostly from African nations, have been scuffling with police and residents in the streets of the Calabrian town of Rosarno since Thursday evening. The violence in the crime-ridden and volatile area started after two immigrants were wounded by unidentified gunmen in an incident that the protesters deemed motivated by racism.

Some 300 African migrants were bused out of a southern Italian town rocked by two days of clashes between the migrants, police and local residents.

The episodes of violence and hostility are an extreme symptom of the chronic neglect seasonal migrant workers are subjected to in Italy, said Loris de Filippi, Médecins Sans Frontières operational co-ordinator. 'While they are crucial to the labor force in Italian agriculture, they are easily exploited,' he added.

Many of the migrants from Ghana, Nigeria and other African countries have been camping out in tents and cardboard shelters in an abandoned cheese factory with no heating and broken windows on the outskirts of Rosarno. They also alleged they were earning illegally low wages – as little as $30 for a 12-hour day picking citrus fruit and other crops. Despite chronically high unemployment rates in Italy's south, many residents don't want to do the backbreaking seasonal farm work.

Loris de Filippi added: 'Most health conditions our medical team treats are related to their appalling living and working conditions, such as respiratory infections, osteo-muscular pain or gastroenteritis. Year after year, our teams go back to the same areas and witness the same horrible conditions, which we try to alleviate by providing medical humanitarian aid. It is about time Italian authorities take measures to improve the conditions of these workers, respect their dignity and improve their access to healthcare.' ∎

Sources: Adriana Sapone/AP 'Migrants bused from riot-struck Italian town', January 2010. MSF PRESS RELEASE, 'Violence in Southern Italy exposes extreme neglect and exploitation of seasonal migrant workers', 12 Jan 2010.

protected from exploitation by recognizing domestic work as formal employment. And there should be a renewed commitment to vigorously combat human trafficking and to protect the rights of trafficked persons, with governments ratifying international conventions to protect the rights of all migrant workers and members of their families.[13]

The greening of anti-immigration

Traditionally, most anti-immigration has fixated on race and culture. Oxford demography professor David Coleman, who advises Migration Watch, has long argued for restriction of immigration on cultural, social and ethnic grounds. A member of the former Eugenics Society, now renamed the Galton Institute, Coleman has projected likely changes in ethnic and racial composition of societies in seven rich world countries.

'The countries of the West,' says Coleman, 'are facilitating a radical transformation of the composition of their societies and the cessation of a specific heritage. Democratic approval might have been thought necessary for so notable and permanent a change, the prospect of which would have been dismissed as absurd just a few decades ago.'[14]

US anthropologist, Virginia Abernethy, a self-avowed 'ethnic separatist', argues that the ability to migrate to rich countries gives people in poor countries an incentive to have bigger families. She has called for a complete moratorium on immigration to the US and says that 'Third World' immigration brings 'dangerous diseases' to the country.

But increasingly the US anti-immigration lobby is taking on a greenish hue and reaching out to environmentalists. 'The United States will not be able to achieve any meaningful reductions in CO_2 emissions without serious economic and social consequences for American citizens unless immigration is sharply curtailed,' claims a recent report by the Federation for American Immigration Reform (FAIR).

Now the argument is: immigrants should be kept out of rich countries because the rich country way of life is a threat to the *global* environment. It's a cunning twist and it forms the basis of a briefing from the right-wing US Center for Immigration Studies (CIS), an offshoot of FAIR which is alleged to have ties with white supremacist groups and funders. The CIS argues that immigration worsens CO_2 emissions because it transfers population from lower-polluting parts of the world to the higher-polluting US.[8]

Population expert and environmentalist Betsy Hartmann disagrees. 'The argument that it's better to keep poor people in poor countries so they consume less is just plain wrong on a number of counts. First, it diverts attention from the urgent need to address over-consumption. Whatever the rate of immigration, well-off Americans need to change their lifestyles for the future of the planet.

'Second, the assumption that immigrating to the US necessarily turns people into super-consumers is a spurious one. Many immigrant communities bring with them traditions of greater respect for the environment. In my hometown of Amherst, Cambodian immigrants helped spur a revival in community gardens. In nearby Holyoke, Puerto Rican immigrants are revitalizing the depressed city in one of the most successful urban renewal and agriculture projects in the country.

'Third, protecting the environment does not mean you have to keep people poor. Contrary to anti-immigrant rhetoric, it's possible to raise incomes and improve the environment at the same time. In the US "green jobs" and "green recovery" programs represent a win-win strategy... '

The anti-immigrant movement has only one solution for global warming: stop immigration. Its response to climate change, Hartmann argues, is 'not all that different from climate deniers who claim global warming isn't a problem and we should just go on consuming fossil fuels the good old American way'.[15]

Nick Griffin, a leading light of the fascist British National Party, exemplifies this. He claims his is the 'only truly green party' because it opposes immigration – while also managing to be a climate change skeptic.

American immigrant-rights campaigner Patricia Huang posits: 'The relationship between population growth and environmental destruction is shaped by how we use our resources, not by the number of people using them.' There's more on population and climate change in the next chapter.

The biggest migration is to come?

Migration is the wildest of cards. Predicting migration flows, demographers are quick to point out, is practically impossible. Most often they are related to violent conflict. The instability in global markets set off by the 2008 credit crisis has thrown another spanner at the crystal ball.

But, according to some pundits, the biggest movement of people is yet to come – and it will be caused by something world leaders are especially adept at ignoring. They have had plenty of warning. As early as 1990 the Intergovernmental Panel on Climate Change stated that 'one of the gravest effects of climate change may be that on human migration'.

Despite the shortage of hard data, it is evident that environmental changes are already resulting in substantial human migration and displacement. In May 2009 rising sea levels finally forced the 2,500 inhabitants of the low-lying Carteret Islands to evacuate their Pacific home and relocate to Bougainville. In the popular press they were described as 'the first victims of climate change'.

Other small island nations facing a similar fate

In the beginning our roof was very high

On the Pacific island of Kiribati, locals already complain that the water has become undrinkable due to salinization. These days, when Oreba Oblin takes a step out of her home, she walks into the sea. The water is rising, she says, explaining that she and her husband have already had to add sand to their home's floor several times to keep it dry. 'In the beginning our roof was very high. Now the roof is getting very close to us. If we keep adding sand to the floor, my head will soon touch the ceiling.'

She has tried to combat coastal erosion by planting mangrove seedlings. Many inhabitants have built sea walls along the shoreline but if the sea continues to rise the sea walls won't suffice.

'We want to stay here... but if we have to move, then we have no choice,' she says.

Kiribati consist of 33 atolls, tiny specks of narrow land made of coral, sand and limestone and barely three meters above sea level. There is no higher land to retreat to.

Leaving means emigrating, forever.

But where will Oreba and thousands like her go? How will they survive and keep their culture alive? ■

Source: UNFPA, *State of World Population 2009*

are Kiribati, Tuvalu, the Marshall Islands and the Maldives.

The UN State of World Population 2009 report notes that: 'Recorded natural disasters have doubled from around 200 to 400 a year over the past two decades. Seven out of ten disasters were recorded as "climate-related". Women and children were the most likely to lose their lives in these disasters. The number of people affected has tripled, with an average of 211 million people directly affected a year.

'Estimating the number of people forced to migrate due to climate change presents a challenge, with figures ranging wildly from 50 million to one billion people by the middle of the century. The movement may be within countries, across borders, on a permanent or temporary basis. The most widely used estimate of people displaced by environmental factors by 2050 is 200 million.'[16]

Frontline Bangladesh

Fly into Dhaka by night and you might think the world had turned upside down. Down below, a spangled galaxy of lights dances in the darkness. As you descend and prepare to land the inky darkness becomes water, the lights, signs of habitation on the many islands and promontories that make up the delta. Such a profusion of human life – in an environment that is wondrous and precarious in equal measure!

Bangladesh has an estimated 162 million people squeezed into an area of 145,000 square kilometers, giving it one of the highest population densities in the world.

To an attentive audience, Vigya Sharma from the University of Adelaide is showing a map of the country projected onto a big screen. She is talking about the way in which climate change is likely to affect its growing population.

Her presentation is not just couched in, it's almost smothered by, academic caution. 'It's hard to predict... Migration is a very complex process... The exact degree with which climate change impacts is not clear...'

But gradually the map tells its own story. The light blue area is that affected by river flooding – and it is enormous, covering most of the inland part of the map. Not surprising when you consider Bangladesh's position at the confluence of three major river systems: the Ganges, the Brahmaputra and the Meghna.

Most of the land-mass lies fewer than 10 meters above sea level, with considerable areas at sea level, leading to frequent and prolonged flooding during the monsoon seasons. Already, rising sea-level is causing yet more flooding as storm surges rise, pushing further inland. These inland areas are home to the poorest people, those most vulnerable to change and least well-equipped to adapt to it. There are a great many of them. Despite the drift to the cities, more than 75 per cent of the country's people still live in rural areas.[1]

The pale green on Vigya Sharma's map shows the coastal areas affected by sea rise. Here, salt-water is already entering freshwater aquifers and estuaries, contaminating drinking water and farmland. A one-meter rise in sea-level – not as improbable as it once seemed – would shrink the country by 18 per cent.

Then there are typhoons, cyclones and storms, made more intense by warmer ocean water, to contend with. Not for nothing did this country top the Global Climate Risk Index of 2009, followed by North Korea and Nicaragua.

Sharma concludes that 'approximately' 99.9 per cent of the country and 100 per cent of the population will suffer from these various effects. And with the population predicted to rise to 240 million by 2050, the future looks even more daunting.

Escape routes

'Suggestions that millions of environmental migrants are poised to flee developing countries to permanently seek safety and new lives in industrialized countries are misleading,' says the UN Population Fund.[16]

It goes on: 'Overall, environmental migration is – and is likely to continue to be – mainly an internal phenomenon, with a smaller proportion of movement taking place between neighboring countries, and even smaller numbers migrating long distances beyond the region of origin.'

For rural Bangladeshis, however, upping sticks and heading to the cities might not be such a workable proposition if the cities in question are coastal ones battling a rising sea. The ensuing loss of land can only intensify existing social and economic pressures.

'We can expect that with increased landlessness due to climate change in Bangladesh,' says Sharma, 'people will use established social networks to move along corridors to other places.'

Bangladesh does have a wide network of communities around the world and many established routes of migration to them. The Middle East, Canada, Australia, Britain, India and some countries of the European Union are the most likely destinations.

But, given the choice, the vast majority of people would rather stay at home and find ways of adapting to their changing environment. Adaptation on a limited scale is already happening. For example, some coastal farmers are growing vegetables on raised beds to mitigate erosion and avoid pollution by sea water. But adaptation costs money – in a country where poverty remains widespread and around 39 per cent of children under five are malnourished.[17]

Unprepared

Bangladesh is reaping the ills sown by others, the rich polluting nations who are the major emitters of greenhouse gases. Back at the 1997 Kyoto climate summit, it was agreed to set up a UN climate change adaptation fund. But donors have been glacially slow to stump up the cash. Spain was the first country to make a significant contribution, of $60 million in April 2010. The first two programs, one in Senegal and one in Honduras, got the go-ahead five months later. The Fund is still far short of the sum required. It is estimated that by 2030 poor countries will need between $28 billion and $59 billion a year to adapt.[18]

In a separate agreement, the government of Bangladesh is due to receive help in supporting vulnerable communities as they adapt to climate change. Initial grant contributions are $1.6 million from Denmark, $10.4 million from the European Union, $11.5 million from Sweden and $86.7 million from Britain. The money is being channeled through the World Bank rather than the UN.[19]

For its part, the World Bank is offering climate adaptation funds in the form of loans rather than grants to poor countries – putting those countries further in debt to the rich world for problems created by the rich world.

The Jubilee Debt Campaign explains: 'For instance, the total package given to Bangladesh is $624 million, of which 92 per cent comes in the form of loans. Over $150 million of the money for these loans has come from the UK government. Ultimately these loans mean the poor will pay twice for climate change.'

Bangladesh obviously needs the best in modern flood defense technology. But also of primary importance is the development of climate-resistant agriculture as local farmers struggle with the double whammy of increased water-salination – caused by rising sea levels – and shortage of fresh water as the Himalayan glaciers that feed the great river systems shrink.

'The impact of climate change on agriculture is undeniable and will most certainly worsen if governments and donors fail to take appropriate steps right now,' warns Ghulam Mohammad Panaullah, former research director of the Bangladesh Rice Research Institute. Already, in coastal areas, cocoa and betel nut trees do not yield half as much as two decades ago, while banana groves are dying out in their hundreds. Vegetables sold in the urban markets of Dhaka, Khulna and Rajshai are rendered tasteless by salt water and fetch low prices.[20]

Much is lacking, at every level, and no-one, it seems, is prepared for what is to come. According to the UNFPA: 'Relief organizations, policy-makers, donors, host nations and affected countries themselves are ill-equipped for environmentally induced population movements, partly because of a shortage of credible data and forecasts, which are essential for raising awareness and mobilizing the political will and resources needed to tackle emerging challenges.'

As she leaves the hall, I ask Vigya Sharma whether she or any of her research colleagues have looked at the connection between population and environment the other way around. That is to say: the impact of population growth on the environment. 'No,' she says. 'But thank you. It's a good subject for a future project.'

I don't think that the environmental activists crying out for population reduction would be very impressed with that answer. In the next chapter we will look at what they have to say.

1 http://nin.tl/egHsMz   2 http://nin.tl/g9kCil   3 Migration Watch UK, www.migrationwatchuk.org 4 The Economist, 'Hot, Dry and Crowded', 6-12 Feb 2010. 5 http://nin.tl/fkhozV 6 Stephen Lunn and Annabel Hepworth, 'Reject little Australia: PM advisers', The Australian, 22 Jul 2010. 7 http://nin.tl/i7qD8m 8 Ian Angus and Simon Butler, 'Should Climate Activists Support Limits on Immigration,' Monthly Review, 25 Jan 2010. 9 Hania Zlotnik, UN Population Division, UN, New York, 27 Oct 2010. 10 UN Population Division, Oct 2009, www.unmigration.org 11 AFP, 'DHS: 7 per cent fewer illegals living in US', 10 Feb 2010. 12 Bob Hughes, 'Too many of whom, and too much of what?' No-One is Illegal discussion paper. 13 Statement of the Global Migration Group, Global Forum on Migration and Development, 4-5 Nov 2009, Athens. 14 David Coleman, 'Immigration and ethnic change in low-fertility countries', (abstract) www.popcouncil.org/EthnicChange. 15 Betsy Hartmann, 'The Greening of Hate: An Environmentalist's Essay', Jul 2010. 16 UNFPA, State of the World's Population 2009, New York 2009. 17 Simon Angus et al, 'Climate change impacts and adaptation in Bangladesh', Monash University, Jul 2009. 18 IRIN news, 'Climate Change: adaptation fund starts delivering', 24 Sep 2010. 19 Gurumia.com 'Climate Change Resilience Fund was established, Oct 2010. 20 IRIN, 'Bangladesh: battling the effects of climate change', Dhaka, 16 Dec 2008.

7 Population and climate change

More people equals more CO$_2$ emissions. So fewer people must equal less global warming. The logic seems unassailable. The connection between population growth and global warming is a subject of growing interest. But could it be an almighty red herring? Or do the people insisting on it have a point?

WHAT'S THE POINT of countries struggling to meet their carbon targets if global population keeps increasing? Shouldn't we be doing something about population?

This is the subject of hot debate today, so let's start with two very different viewpoints, both from within the environmental movement.

First, that of the respected British environmental campaigner Jonathon Porritt, Founder Director of Forum for the Future. He is also a supporter of the Optimum Population Trust, which seeks to limit population growth.

Second, the view from The Corner House, an equally respected British-based organization that aims to support democratic and community movements for environmental and social justice and which has produced research papers on both climate and population issues.

Here's what Jonathon Porritt has to say:
It astonishes me that population remains such a controversial issue when there is so much to agree on from a progressive, radical perspective:

We would all agree that it would be a better world for women if they were able to manage their own fertility, including access to safe, reliable and cheap contraception.

We would all agree that it would be a better world if all women had access to improved healthcare (particularly reproductive healthcare), and if all girls had the right to be in education for as long as boys are.

And I suspect the vast majority would agree that there is a clear link between high population growth in many countries and the continuing failure to address life-crushing poverty in those countries.

But fewer, I suspect, would subscribe to the overall conclusion which emerged from the latest report of the British All Party Parliamentary Group on Population, Development and Reproductive Health (APPG):

'The failure to prioritize family planning in overseas development aid is resulting in population growth levels that present a serious threat to health, economic development and the environment in some of the world's poorest countries. Urgent action must be taken to ensure family-planning provision becomes an integral part of all efforts to reduce poverty, and improve mothers' and children's survival and health.'

No doubt the APPG would have had in mind countries like Bangladesh (where the population has grown from 71 million in 1974 to 162 million today, with a fertility rate of 3 children per woman) and Ethiopia. Twenty-five years ago at the time of the terrible famine, Ethiopia's population was around 34 million. Now it's 72 million. Spending on family planning has declined steadily over the last decade. And famine is back.

For me, there is a compelling humanitarian case for full-on support for family planning in those countries dogged by that crushing combination of high average fertility and dire poverty. But, on top of all that, we've now got to take climate change into account. And that means taking into account not just total emissions of greenhouse gases, but the total number of emitters.

At one level, this is all about basic mathematics. We roughly know the total volume of greenhouse gases we can put into the atmosphere over the next few decades if we are to stay the right side of the two-degree-centigrade increase (by the end of the century) which scientists tell us we absolutely mustn't go above. That total volume has to be divided up between the total amount of people doing the emitting.

And that's where we have to take China into account. The outcome of China's one-child family policy (however abhorrent it may be from a human rights perspective) is that 400 million births have been 'averted'.

On average, each citizen of China emits around 4.5 tonnes of CO_2 per annum. That would have been an additional 1.5 billion tonnes of CO_2 emitted per annum, give or take a few hundred thousand tonnes, if those births had not been averted.

My friends in Greenpeace and Friends of the Earth hate this logical, mathematical exercise. And that's because they are foolish enough to suppose that all effective family-planning exercises have to be done China-style. They don't. They can be done Kerala-style, or Thailand-style or Iran-style – where equally rapid reductions in the fertility rate have been achieved via better education, better healthcare, better access to contraception and inspired government and community leadership.

But the reasons for the continuing non-engagement of the big environment groups are deeper than this. They have a very deep fear that addressing population issues will distract people from the real issue: over-consumption in the rich world rather than overpopulation in the poor world. This is stupid. It really is possible to pursue two big issues at the same time! What's more, today's poor countries all want to be tomorrow's richer countries, at which point their emissions may not look so very different from those in the rich world today.

Beyond that, there are all sorts of fears that

addressing population issues will get them tangled up in gritty controversies around immigration, the role of religion, and complex cultural factors such as continuing male domination in many countries with high fertility rates.

On that score, they are absolutely right. Of course there are a lot of nasty, extremist voices out there, only too happy to use the population debate to advance their own inhumane and racist views. But they won't go away just because the rest of us stay silent.

Whichever way you cut this one, I believe it's part of our duty to the next generation, not just to promote this debate – but to advance the compassionate, progressive case for a full-on global campaign to put the world on a downward population trajectory just as fast as we can.[1]

And here's what the Corner House says:
The burning of fossil fuels to drive a century and a half of Western industrialization is by far the major contributor to human-caused climate change. This is unsustainable.

There is simply not enough 'space' in above-ground biological and geological systems to park safely the huge mass of carbon coming out of the ground without carbon dioxide building up catastrophically in both the air and the oceans. The earth and its ecosystems undeniably have limits.

At the most fundamental level, therefore, the climate solution requires turning away from fossil fuel dependence.

It is not surprising, however, that a worsening climate situation is often attributed not to continued fossil-fuel extraction but to too many people. Whenever global environmental crises, Third World poverty or world hunger are at issue, whenever conflict, migration or economic growth are discussed, economists, demographers, political pundits and others frequently invoke overpopulation.

Today, a range of industries use the spuriously neutral mathematics of overpopulation arguments to colonize the future for their particular interests and to privatize public resources. In agriculture, the talk is of extra mouths in the South causing global famine – unless biotechnology companies have the right to patent and genetically engineer seeds.

With respect to water, it is asserted that growing numbers of thirsty slum dwellers will threaten water wars – unless water resources are handed over to private-sector water companies. And in climate, the talk is of teeming Chinese and Indians causing whole cities to be lost to flooding through their greenhouse gas emissions – unless polluting companies are granted property rights in the atmosphere through carbon-trading schemes and carbon offsets. These are the tools of the main official approach to the climate crisis that aims to build a global carbon market worth trillions of dollars.

Numerous studies highlight the contradictions in correlating population growth with carbon emissions, both historical and predicted. Industrialized countries, with only 20 per cent of the world's population, are responsible for 80 per cent of the accumulated carbon dioxide in the atmosphere. The countries with the highest greenhouse gas emissions are those with slow or declining population growth. The few countries in the world where birth rates remain high have the lowest per capita carbon emissions.

And even aggregate figures for per capita emissions still tend to obscure just who is producing greenhouse gases and how, by statistically leveling out emissions among everyone.

Population numbers, in sum, offer no useful pointers toward policies that should be adopted to tackle climate change. Massive fossil-fuel use *in industrialized societies cannot be countered by handing out condoms. Nor will reducing the number of births dent the massive annual subsidies, estimated at over $100 billion, that oil companies receive in tax breaks, giving them an unfair advantage over low-carbon alternatives. Nor will population policies stop carbon trading, which gives incentives to polluting industries in North and South to delay making structural changes away from the extraction and use of fossil fuels while usurping land, water and air on which Southern communities depend.*

But facts, figures and alternative explanations, while necessary, have never had much effect on population debates because, deep down, they are less about numbers than about power, economic interests, rights, markets and welfare. They are political and cultural disagreements, not mathematical ones.

Solutions to the climate crisis depend first and foremost on political organizing and on social and economic changes. We need to adopt structurally different, non-fossil energy, transport, agricultural and consumption regimes within a few decades to minimize future dangers and costs. Infrastructure, trade, even community structure, will have to be reorganized and state support shifted toward popular movements that are already constructing or defending low-carbon means of livelihood and social life.

Discussions about overpopulation distract from these priorities. Because they obscure relationships of power between different groups in societies while justifying relationships that allow some to dominate others, they serve to delay making these structural changes. They also serve to explain away the failure of carbon markets to tackle the problem. And, finally, they serve to justify more interventions in the countries deemed to hold the surplus people – and to excuse those interventions when they cause further environmental degradation, migration or conflict.'[1]

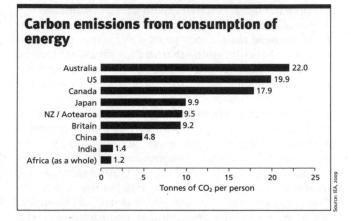

Carbon emissions from consumption of energy

Country	Tonnes of CO_2 per person
Australia	22.0
US	19.9
Canada	17.9
Japan	9.9
NZ / Aotearoa	9.5
Britain	9.2
China	4.8
India	1.4
Africa (as a whole)	1.2

Source: IEA, 2009

So, both have had their say. What are we to make of the differences between these perspectives?

The view that population size is a core problem makes sense to many people despairing about climate change. The political will to tackle climate change – technologically, economically, politically – has shown itself to be pitifully weak. Emerging from years of political exile comes the notion of 'population control' – and it comes dressed like a solution of sorts.

Organizations such as the Sierra Club and Population Connection in the US, and the Optimum Population Trust (OPT) in Britain, have successfully tapped into public anxiety and the need to 'do' something. Just prior to the 2009 Copenhagen Climate Summit, the OPT launched Pop Offsets. This invited people in the rich world to offset their own carbon emissions by funding family planning in the Global South.

The campaign has been strongly criticized for giving out quite the wrong kind of message. Many will interpret Pop Offsets as meaning 'if we can stop *them* having babies then we won't have to change *our* ways'.

The ethics of promoting family planning in the Global South as a means of trying to reduce climate damage are questionable. But so are the mathematics. They just don't add up, say experts who have been looking more closely.

Brian O'Neill and his team at the National Center for Atmospheric Research, Boulder, Colorado, have been scrutinizing the impact of population on energy consumption, land use and climate change. Their work has involved examining how differently the three UN population projections (low 8, medium 9, high 11 billion) would affect CO_2 emissions.

In late 2009 O'Neill's colleague Leiwen Jiang reported that the different sizes of population made a difference that was 'substantial but not decisive'.

He explained: 'We need to reduce emissions by seven billion tonnes by 2050. But population growth difference [between different projections] only makes a difference of one or plus-one or minus-one billion tonnes, because most of the population growth will be in the developing countries. Developed countries are the ones that make a far larger contribution to CO_2 than to population size because of comparatively much higher contribution to greenhouse gases.'[2]

Put another way, if the population were to reach, say, 7.4 billion in 2050 instead of, say, the 8.9 billion currently projected, it would reduce emissions by only 15 per cent.[3] This is not nearly enough to meet even the most modest current targets. The G8's target is for a global reduction of 'at least 50 per cent' by 2050, and in 2009 it recognized that the countries of the G8 had to cut their emissions by 80 per cent by 2050.[4]

Furthermore, thanks to its prolonged economic boom, carbon emissions from fossil fuels are growing fastest in China as it produces consumer items for the world. But fertility there is already below replacement.

Population is growing fastest in sub-Saharan Africa where emissions per person are only a fraction of what they are in the US. So reducing population growth there would have little effect on climate.

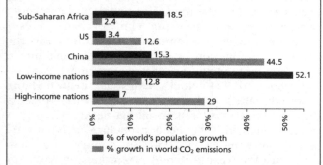

The weakest link – population growth and CO₂

David Satterthwaite analyzed changes in population and in greenhouse-gas emissions for all the world's countries and found the following results for the period between 1980 and 2005.

- Sub-Saharan Africa: 18.5 / 2.4
- US: 3.4 / 12.6
- China: 15.3 / 44.5
- Low-income nations: 52.1 / 12.8
- High-income nations: 7 / 29

■ % of world's population growth
■ % growth in world CO₂ emissions

Population growth rates in China have come down rapidly – but greenhouse-gas emissions have increased equally rapidly.

Most of the nations with the highest population growth rates had low growth rates for carbon-dioxide emissions while many of the nations with the lowest population growth rates had high growth rates for carbon-dioxide emissions. ■

Source: IIED, Sep 2009

This tallies with the findings of David Satterthwaite at the London-based International Institute for Environment and Development, who finds, at most, a weak link between population growth and rising emissions of the greenhouse gases that cause climate change[5] (see above).

So unequal are global consumption levels that one European or North American or Australian may be responsible for more emissions than an entire village of Africans.[6]

Is it up to richer people in the rich world, then, to have fewer children or none at all? Well, it might help in countries like the US which has a higher than replacement fertility rate and is (along with Australia) top of the league of per capita polluters [see chart page 98]. But it won't make enough difference because it fails to tackle the real underlying issue of how we live.

As Simon Butler, writing in Australia's *Green Left Weekly*, puts it: 'People are not pollution. Blaming too many people for driving climate change is like blaming too many trees for causing bushfires. The real cause of climate change is an economy locked into burning fossil fuels for energy and unsustainable agriculture.'[7]

There's no dodging it. We need an energy revolution – away from fossil fuels and towards renewables – which is as radical as and more rapid than the industrial revolution that laid the basis for our carbon-based economies. And we need it regardless of how big the population gets.

'Those who say the whole problem is population are wrong,' says leading US demographer Joel Cohen. 'It's not even the dominant factor.'[3]

But there are other problems associated with growing populations. For example, how are we going to feed nine billion of us?

1 First appeared in *New Internationalist*, NI 430, Jan-Feb 2010. 2 Leiwen Jiang, IUSSP Conference: Session 170, Marrakech, 2009. 3 Robert Kunzig, 'Population 7 Billion', *National Geographic*, Jan 2011. 4 America.gov 9 July 2009 5 David Satterthwaite, 'The implications of population growth on urbanization and climate change', *Environment and Urbanization*, Sep 2009. 6 Fred Pearce, 'Population: Over-consumption is the real problem', *New Scientist*, 23 Sep 2009. 7 Simon Butler, 'Ten reasons why population control can't stop climate change', *Green Left* online, 31 May, 2009, www.greenleft.org.au

8 How can we feed nine billion?

Not enough food, not enough water, not enough... Fears of scarcity are often at the heart of population anxiety, but recent food crises are making matters look serious.

WHEN THOMAS ROBERT MALTHUS signaled his fear of population growth – and of having to share society's wealth more equitably – the issue he focused on was very basic: hunger. It was in the nature of population growth, he said, that it would inevitably outstrip the availability of land and therefore food.

His story was proved wrong, and he later admitted he had made up his mathematical correlation between the two. Population grew, farming methods improved, food imports from other countries increased, and England didn't starve.

Indeed, centuries later and in a far wider context, development economist Amartya Sen went so far as to say that he could think of no famine that had been caused by population pressure, but plenty that had resulted from inequality and failures of distribution.

More recently, however, the question is being posed: Malthus may have been wrong in his own lifetime, but is he right in ours?

An influential scientific report on global food and farming produced by Foresight, the British government's futures thinktank, sounded a warning in early 2011.

Professor Sir John Beddington, the government's chief scientific adviser and head of the Foresight program, said: 'The study shows that the food system is already failing in at least two ways. First, it is unsustainable, with resources being used faster than they can be naturally replenished. Second, a billion people are going hungry with another billion people suffering from "hidden hunger", whilst a billion

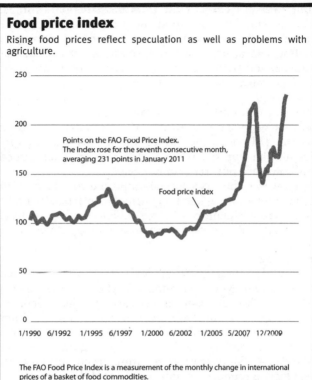

Food price index

Rising food prices reflect speculation as well as problems with agriculture.

Points on the FAO Food Price Index.
The Index rose for the seventh consecutive month, averaging 231 points in January 2011

Food price index

1/1990 6/1992 1/1995 6/1997 1/2000 6/2002 1/2005 5/2007 12/2009

The FAO Food Price Index is a measurement of the monthly change in international prices of a basket of food commodities.
Rising food prices reflect speculation on food commodities as well as problems with agriculture.

Source: UN World Food Program, 2.2011

people are over-consuming.'

The report, entitled *Global Food and Farming Futures*, predicts that the world will need 70 to 100 per cent more food to feed a population of nine billion by 2050. The amount of arable land, however, is likely to remain static. It may even shrink, thanks to effects of climate change such as drought, flooding and rising sea levels.[1]

Up until 2008 the idea that the world might not be

able to feed itself was far from most people's minds. Overproduction and 'food mountains' had been the more common problems in many countries.

But, during the 2008 food crisis, prices of staples shot up and there were riots in 32 countries.

The causes were variously ascribed: commodity speculation, drought in Australia and biofuels. In the year from 2007 to 2008 up to 95 million tons of cereals were manufactured into biofuels. According to the IMF and the World Bank this was mainly responsible for the spike in food prices that tipped millions into poverty and hunger.[2]

However, the UN's special rapporteur on the right to food, Olivier de Schutter, concluded in late 2010 that financial speculation – in particular, trading in food commodity derivatives – had played a major role.[3]

Faultlines

The 2008 crisis revealed deep flaws in the global food system. Most alarming was the extent to which Majority World countries had become dependent on food imports from the industrial world. This had not come about by accident. The global regime of 'free trade' overseen by the World Trade Organization had allowed richer countries to dump their agricultural produce on poorer countries at rock-bottom prices that put local producers out of business. In many cases the dumped food had been grown with subsidies from rich-world governments.

African farming, in particular, suffered. What was the point of growing tomatoes in Ghana if the market was flooded with cheap imports from Italy? Over the years, less and less foreign development aid had been going towards developing food production in Africa. In 1980 farming received 20 per cent of the African aid budget; by 2006 it was only 4 per cent. African governments had also cut their own investment in agriculture to just five per cent on average.[4]

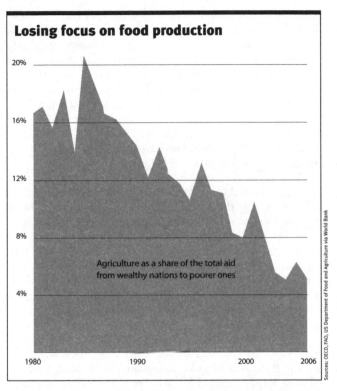

Losing focus on food production

20%

16%

12%

8%

Agriculture as a share of the total aid
from wealthy nations to poorer ones

4%

1980   1990   2000   2006

Sources: OECD, FAO, US Department of Food and Agriculture via World Bank

It is often said that 'Africa can't feed itself' – and this is now repeated in the context of a predicted doubling of the continent's population by 2050. But when US demographer Barbara Boyle Torrey of the Population Reference Bureau did a simple calculation of the number of calories currently harvested on the continent in relation to the number of people, she made a surprising discovery. Although productivity per hectare is about a quarter of what it could be, Africa currently produces enough calories, in theory, to feed its people.[5]

In practice, even in the midst of a famine, a poor

country may export food – as Ethiopia did in 1984. Today, food security in Africa could be about to take a serious turn for the worse. Foreign interests are rushing to buy up large expanses of arable land in the Majority World. Governments and private investors from Europe, the US, China, Korea, and the Middle East have been on shopping sprees. China has acquired at least 1.2 million hectares in the Philippines, and more land in Laos and Kenya. The Abu Dhabi Fund for Development has brought up 30,000 fertile hectares in Sudan.[4]

People who have been tilling their fields for generations suddenly find that their government has sold or leased the terrain they thought was theirs to private investors and foreign governments for decades to come.

This is what happened to subsistence farmers in the remote West African village of Soumouni in Mali. One day, six strangers turned up to tell them that their humble fields were now controlled by Libya's then leader, Colonel Muammar el-Qaddafi, and that they would have to leave.

'They told us this would be the last rainy season for us to cultivate our fields; after that, they will level all the houses and take the land,' said village leader Mama Keita, aged 73. 'We were told that Qaddafi owns this land.'[6]

According to a World Bank study there were farmland deals for at least 44.5 million hectares during the first 11 months of 2009 alone. More than 70 per cent were for land in Africa, with Sudan, Mozambique and Ethiopia among those nations transferring millions of hectares to investors. Before the 2008 food crisis, the global average for such deals was less than 4 million hectares per year.

The prospect of future scarcity has attracted the governments of wealthy countries and hedge funds. The World Bank maintains that this could help feed the increasing global population by introducing large-scale commercial farming to places without it.

Others see the deals as little more than neo-colonial land grabs that destroy communities, uprooting tens of thousands of farmers, condemning them to poverty and creating landlessness and hunger. Local people have been pushed off land in Ethiopia, Uganda, the Democratic Republic of Congo, Liberia and Zambia. To make matters worse, much of the food now grown there is bound for wealthier nations.

'The food security of the country concerned must be first and foremost in everybody's mind,' said Kofi Annan, the former United Nations Secretary General who is now working on the issue of African agriculture. 'Otherwise it is straightforward exploitation and it won't work. We have seen a scramble for Africa before. I don't think we want to see a second scramble of that kind.'[7]

It is already too late in some places. Furthermore, some of the investments appear to be pure speculation that leaves land fallow and will not add anything to the world's food stocks. In fact, by driving farmers off the land it will have had the opposite effect.

Trouble ahead

There is no denying that feeding nine billion people looks like quite a challenge in a world where already at least one billion out of seven goes hungry. Water is also in short supply; according to the World Health Organization water shortage affects one in three people on every continent and is getting worse with population growth, urbanization and increased usage by households and industry. Topsoil erosion is another problem: by some estimates a third of the world's fields are losing soil faster than natural processes can create new soils. All these problems are exacerbated by climate change. The US Academy of Sciences reckons that every rise of one degree worldwide will

How can we feed nine billion?

Malthus in Africa?

Population pressure has often been blamed for hunger or conflict. The British, for example, preferred to use 'overpopulation' as an explanation for 19th-century potato famines in Ireland rather than to deal with rural people's lack of access to huge areas of land held by absentee landlords.

More recently, overpopulation has been given as the underlying cause for the 1994 Rwandan genocide, in which around 800,000 Tutsi (traditionally cattle-herding) people were murdered by the country's Hutu (traditionally farming) majority. The argument is that population pressure 'cooks up' the genocide. But is it true? asks environmental writer and journalist Fred Pearce.

'Rwanda is certainly densely populated,' he writes. 'Fertility is high at 8.5 per woman, though on the eve of the massacre it had fallen to 6.2. But nobody was starving. The food grown per head was actually growing. But by 1985 all land outside national parks was being cultivated. Young people were having difficulty getting land. Wealthy northern Hutu élites and their allies had been busy increasing their estates in the 1970s and 1980s. So the people who had the land committed the massacres, not the landless. Rising population aggravated tensions but Rwanda has a large population because it is very fertile. It can sustain one. Throughout the 1970s and 1980s it was one of Africa's top agricultural performers. Food production rose by 4.7 per cent for almost two decades, easily outpacing population growth. On the eve of the massacre, Rwanda was one of the best-fed countries in central Africa, with more than 2,000 calories per person per day. Hunger was not the trigger, nor environmental degradation.... Other things were making Rwandans poor. The ongoing war that had been... causing migration instability. And the price of coffee was halved in 1989 as price controls were swept away in the name of free trade. I have never heard the free market of coffee mentioned as an explanation for the Rwandan genocide, but arguably it was much more important than growing population.' ∎

Source: Fred Pearce, *Peoplequake*, Eden Project Books, 2010.

cut corn, rice and wheat yields by 10 per cent.[4]

The Foresight report says that feeding a much bigger world population by 2050 will require a sharp increase in yields – similar to those during the controversial, socially and environmentally damaging, 'green revolution' of the 1960s and 1970s. It adds that, to boost crop yields to the level needed to provide enough food for all, every scientific tool must be considered, including the use of genetically modified

(GM) crops – which have been largely rejected by European consumers.

'We say very clearly that we should not tie our hands behind our backs by dismissing GM,' said one of the report's authors.

This is music to the ears of the biotech industry, which has been lobbying hard to promote GM as a solution to the food crisis, population growth and climate change.

'That dramatic drop in yield is just a foreshadowing of the challenges that lie ahead for agriculture during the 21st century, as temperatures rise and another three billion people are added to the global population,' says University of California Davis plant pathologist Pamela Ronald. 'The good news is that we have the ability, through conventional breeding and genetic engineering, to generate new varieties of our existing food crops that can better adapt to these environmental changes.'[7]

Ellen Kullman, Chair and CEO of the US chemical company DuPont, told business and political leaders meeting at the 2011 World Economic Forum in Davos that there were 'vast opportunities' for industrial biotechnology to address challenges resulting from population growth.[8]

Environmental researchers at The Corner House doubt such business opportunities will benefit humanity: 'The biotechnology industry claims that genetic engineering in agriculture is necessary to feed a growing world population. Yet, far from preventing world starvation, genetic engineering threatens to exacerbate the social and ecological causes of hunger by forcing farmers to pay for their right to fertile seeds, threatening crop yields, undermining biodiversity and reducing the access of poorer people to food.'[9]

Besides, there are other non-GM, low-tech options.

How can we feed nine billion?

Better farming

Current world food production is grossly inefficient. Millions of liters of water are wasted each year by conventional methods of flooding fields to irrigate crops. If these were replaced with simple drip-irrigation systems, most of the world's farmers could halve their water use. In Africa yields can be multiplied in comparatively simple ways. In Malawi, for example, the 2005 harvest was doubled in one year when the government handed out better seeds and fertilizers following a drought.

Agricultural expert Bob Watson reckons farm yields in Africa could be increased from a typical one tonne per hectare to five tonnes 'using today's technology'. It's not a technological challenge, he says, but a 'rural development challenge'.[4]

The scientists contributing to the Foresight report believe that crop yields should be increased by 'sustainable intensification'. This means improving the efficiency of food production without incurring the negative side-effects on the environment seen in the first 'green revolution'.

This may sound good but large-scale agriculture has too often been accompanied by the most environmentally damaging of methods, including high pesticide use. Turning over Africa's fields to industrial agribusiness is unlikely to result in the 'sustainable intensification' called for.

The US based Worldwatch Institute wants a different approach. It believes that the key to alleviating world hunger, poverty and combating climate change lies in new, small-scale approaches to agriculture. Its 2011 report gives examples of community-based initiatives in urban farming, school gardening and indigenous livestock preservation that are working towards poverty relief in an environmentally sustainable way.

For example, in the populous Nairobi slum of Kibera, local women are cultivating vertical gardens

The vertical farm

Indoor vertical farms, many storeys high, could be situated even in the heart of the world's towns and cities. They offer the promise of urban renewal, sustainable production of a safe and varied food supply and the eventual repair of ecosystems that have been sacrificed to horizontal farming.

Here are some of the advantages:

- Year-round crop production: one indoor hectare is equivalent to 4-6 outdoor hectares or more, depending upon the crop
- No weather-related crop failures due to droughts, floods, pests
- All food is grown organically: no herbicides, pesticides, or fertilizers
- Recycling used water virtually eliminates agricultural runoff
- Allows farmland to return to nature, restoring ecosystem functions and services
- Greatly reduces the incidence of infectious diseases
- Adds energy back to the grid via methane generation from composting non-edible parts of plants and animals
- Dramatically reduces fossil-fuel use – no tractors, plows or shipping.
- Converts abandoned urban properties into food production centers
- Creates sustainable environments and employment for urban centers.

Source: The Vertical Farm Project, www.verticalfarm.com

in sacks, providing them with a source of income but also an element of food security for their families. They sell their produce and also consume part of what they grow. The idea of organic 'vertical farms' in urban areas is being developed in the West, too (see opposite).

In rich and poor countries alike, self-sufficiency and waste reduction are better ways to address food security and climate change issues. But, says Worldwatch's Brian Halweil, the majority of government initiatives to farmers 'are still tied to the production mindset. The farmers are rewarded for sheer production quantity, with very little guidance for the quality they produce and the impact of their farming practices on the environment and on human health and nutrition...'[10]

In times of panic over human numbers, perhaps the

most heretical suggestion is that population pressure can sometimes actually improve the environment and its capacity to grow food.

Take the example of Machakos, a rural area east of Nairobi. In the 1930s the area was condemned by British colonial rulers as a treeless, eroded wasteland, thanks to the 'multiplication of the natives'. Some 60 years later its agricultural output had increased tenfold. How? More people, say geographer Michael Mortimore and development consultant Mary Tiffen, who got to know the area well. Population growth meant that there were more mouths to feed, but also more hands to work the fields and improve the land. They dug terraces to reduce soil erosion, created sand dams to capture rainwater, planted trees, raised animals to manure the land and introduced labor-intensive and high-value crops like vegetables.

It's not an isolated case. Damage is often done by growing populations – but often the opposite is true too. Geographer and Oxfam worker Chris Reij has seen it happen on the desert fringes of West Africa and elsewhere. 'The idea that population pressure inevitably leads to increased land degeneration is a much-repeated myth. It does not. Innovation is common in regions where there is high population pressure. This is not surprising. Farmers have to adapt to survive.'[4]

Wasteful habits

Some adaptations are better than others, however. One consequence of economic booms in China and India is the speed with which Western lifestyles are being adopted.

In China people are today consuming four times as much food from animal sources as they were in 1989. Take Han Xiaotao and Cui Xiaona. Migrant workers from the small town of Xingtai in Hebei province, the couple moved to run a butcher stall at a market in western Beijing.

'Life in the countryside is much simpler,' said Han. 'There we ate simple food like noodles, mantou [steamed bread] and corn, and supplied vegetables for the family from our courtyard, things like cucumber, tomatoes, potatoes, cabbage and green onions. When I was young we had only cabbage every day.'

They now regularly enjoy pork, beef and chicken. 'My wife likes fish!' said Han. 'In the countryside, it is too difficult to buy fish. But here it is so easy.'[11]

The world's growing appetite for cars, meat and dairy is setting back its capacity to feed itself in the future. In the first eight years of the new millennium, global grain production grew by 1.2 per cent per year – that's almost the same rate that population grew.

But consumption also increased to meet the world's appetite for biofuels and for meat and dairy products. By 2008 a third of US corn was feeding cars not people. Filling one SUV tank takes as much corn as could feed a person for a year.[4] (Little wonder the then UN special rapporteur on the right to food Jean Ziegler dubs biofuels 'a crime against humanity'.)[2]

Meat and dairy are no better. It takes eight calories of grain to make one calorie of meat. Of the two billion tonnes of grain grown in the world in 2008, under half was eaten directly by people. US demographer Joel Cohen takes an optimistic view – it means, he

---

Meat facts:

Meat production has increased by 500 per cent since 1950. Global meat consumption is expected to grow two per cent each year until 2015, especially in developing countries where eating meat is a sign of prosperity. Half of the world's pork is now eaten in China, while Brazil is the second largest consumer of beef, after the US.

But more and more people – including 150 million in Europe alone – are either becoming vegetarians or reducing their consumption of meat.

Source: Worldwatch Institute, 2010

The fat of the world

Obesity rates worldwide have doubled in the last three decades even as blood pressure and cholesterol levels have dropped.

People in Pacific island nations like American Samoa are the heaviest. Among developed countries, Americans are the fattest and the Japanese are the slimmest.

'Being obese is no longer just a Western problem,' says Majid Ezzati, a professor of public health at Imperial College London.

In 1980, about 5 per cent of men and 8 per cent of women worldwide were obese. By 2008, the rates were nearly 10 per cent for men and 14 per cent for women.

That means 205 million men and 297 million women weigh in as obese. Another 1.5 billion adults are overweight.

Though richer countries do a better job of keeping blood pressure and cholesterol levels under control, researchers say people nearly everywhere are piling on the pounds, except in a few places such as central Africa and South Asia.

Experts warn that the increasing numbers of obese people could lead to a 'global tsunami of cardiovascular disease'. Obesity is also linked to higher rates of cancer and diabetes and is estimated to cause about three million deaths worldwide every year.

Source: *The Lancet*, 4 Feb 2010

---

says, that the world is already growing enough grain to feed 10 billion people, on a vegetarian diet.[4]

A vegetarian diet requires less than half the land of a meaty one, so huge savings could be made if people ate less meat, encouraged perhaps by a green tax that reflected its true environmental cost.

As global population surges, Western tastes for diets rich in meat and dairy products are simply unsustainable, say experts from the United Nations Environment Programme (UNEP), which advocates a shift towards a vegan diet.[12] Such a move would also save water – it takes an unbelievable 990 liters of water to produce one liter of milk.[13]

It's not just India and China that are adding to the world's meaty feast. Thanks partly to fast food, meat consumption is up across the Western world. Britons, for example, are now eating 50 per cent more meat than they were 40 years ago.

There is another way in which we could be managing with far less land: by addressing the scandal of food waste.

Affluent countries waste shocking amounts. About 40 per cent of food bought in them ends up being thrown away. In his exhaustive oeuvre, *Waste: Uncovering the Global Food Scandal*, farmer, writer and activist Tristram Stuart has traced this wastage all along the production and retailing line. For example, farmers often have to grow 25 per cent extra to ensure meeting supermarket contracts and to avoid expensive penalties. Aesthetic standards, overstocking, and sell-by and use-by dates all add to losses. According to government statistics, Britons throw away a third of the food they buy. In the US around 50 per cent of all food is wasted.[2]

While affluent nations throw away food due to greed or neglect, in poorer countries crops rot because farmers lack the means to process, store and transport them to market.

'There is a fantastic amount of slack in the world's food supply, where efficiency measures could create enormous savings, help the fight against hunger and guarantee food for future generations,' writes Stuart.

Poverty and inequality cause further waste. In economically booming India, food rots or gets thrown away while the poor go hungry because they cannot afford to buy it.

Surely tackling issues like these, today, makes more sense than trying to control the number of people who are going to be at the global table in 40 years' time.

The politics of scarcity
There are shortages that threaten the world and the survival of humans within it. But they are primarily scarcities of equity, justice, genuine democracy and respect for nature. Hunger, as we have seen, is rarely

caused by absolute scarcity. Rather it has to do with socially generated scarcity. There is not enough food for some people in some places because other people have the power to deny access to food, land and water. But the fear of scarcity is also being manufactured today by corporations and governments that see business opportunities in doing so.

Some of the very things that are today being presented as solutions to food scarcity – the rich-world takeover of Majority World land for large-scale agribusiness, or the persistent push for genetic modification – are already excluding poor people and pushing them further towards hunger and need. This is only made worse by commodity speculation that turns vital food resources into gambling chips for powerful investors, be they hedge funds, investment banks or pension funds.

Poverty and hunger are the products of grossly unequal power relationships between the haves and the have-nots, regardless of human numbers.

But what about the relationship between humans and the other species with whom we share the planet? That's a tangled issue, as we shall see next.

1 Foresight, *Global Food and Farming Futures*, BIS, Jan 2011. 2 Tristram Stuart, *Waste: Uncovering the Global Food Scandal*, Penguin Books, 2009. 3 Olivier de Schutter, 'Food Commodities Speculation and Food Price Rises', UN, 25 Sept 2010. 4 Fred Pearce, *Peoplequake*, Eden Project Books, 2010. 5 Barbara Boyle Torrey, IUSSP conference: Session 162, Marrakech, 2009. 6 Neil MacFarquhar, 'African Farmers Displaced as Investors Move In', *New York Times*, 21 Dec 2010. 7 Pamela Ronald, University of California Davis, 13 Feb 2010. 8 Advertiser Talk, DuPont Chair & CEO: 'Industrial Biotechnology and Innovation Can Address Challenges Presented from Global Population Growth', 2 Feb 2011. 9 The Corner House, www.cornerhouse.org 10 Worldwatch Institute, 'State of the World 2011: Innovations that Nourish the Planet', Jan 2011. 11 Steve Connor, 'How scientists propose a major policy shift to tackle one of the great challenges of the 21st century', *The Independent*, 22 Jan 2011. 12 Felicity Carus, 'Lesser consumption of animal products is necessary to save the world from the worst impacts of climate change, UN report says', guardian.co.uk, 2 Jun 2010. 13 Caroline Davies, 'Meat by numbers', *Observer*, 7 Sep 2008.

9 Wild things

There's plenty of room for a few billion more humans if we share the earth's resources more equitably. But what about our impact on other species and on the world's biodiversity?

'WRAP WITH CARE... save the polar bear,' reads the slogan on one of the condom wrappers created by the Arizona-based Center for Biological Diversity.

'Hump smarter... save the snail darter,' advises another.

The message is simple: rapid human population growth is pushing other animals out of their habitats and causing species extinction.

'There is a big lacuna in your report,' a reader wrote to me in response to a special feature on population I wrote for *New Internationalist* magazine. 'In a world full of our species, what about diminishing space for other species?'

He had a point. I had actually meant to have a piece on the impact of population growth on biodiversity but this was squeezed out for lack of space. Which seems quite symbolic now.

'US scientists say the Earth is in the midst of its sixth mass extinction of plants and animals, with nearly 50 per cent of all species disappearing,' reads a news agency report. 'Biologists at the University of California-Santa Barbara say they are working to determine which species must be saved.'[1]

In 2008, the International Union for Conservation of Nature (IUCN) updated its Red List inventory of biodiversity and announced that half the world's mammals were declining in population and more than a third probably face extinction.[2]

The actual situation may be worse still because researchers have been unable to classify the threat level for another 836 mammal species due to lack of data.

Wild things

'In reality, the proportion of threatened mammals could be as high as 36 per cent,' IUCN scientist Jan Schipper told the US-based journal *Science*.

The most vulnerable groups are primates, our nearest relatives on the evolutionary ladder, and marine mammals, including several species of whales, dolphins and porpoises.[2] The biggest cause of extinction is habitat loss, and the strongest forces in rapid habitat loss are human beings.

Nearly every region on earth is affected. The loss of microbes in soils that formerly supported tropical forests, the extinction of fish and various aquatic species in polluted habitats, and changes in global climate brought about by the release of greenhouse gases: all these are results of human activity.

How have we done it? We have converted land to agriculture, allowed our towns and cities to sprawl, built roads through fragile ecosystems, drilled for oil and gas, and expanded destructive mining activities. We have cut down forests for logging, polluted lakes, seas and rivers, degraded coral reefs and fragmented the wilderness. And we have

Global figures for 2009 IUCN Red List of Threatened Species:

Total species assessed = 47,677

Total Extinct or Extinct in the Wild = 875 (2%)
   [Extinct = 809; Extinct in the Wild = 66].

Total threatened = 17,291 (36%)
   [Critically Endangered = 3,325; Endangered = 4,891;
   Vulnerable = 9,075].

Total Near Threatened = 3,650 (8%).

Total Lower Risk/conservation dependent = 281 (under 1%)

Total Data Deficient = 6,557 (14%)

Total Least Concern = 19,023 (40%)

Source: IUCN

pumped tonnes and tonnes of greenhouse gases into the atmosphere.

There can be no doubt about which species is holding the smoking gun.

To breed or not to breed

One organization has a radical solution to this state of affairs: it's called the Voluntary Human Extinction Movement or VHEMT (pronounced vehement).

Its founder is Les Knight, a Vietnam vet and former member of Zero Population Growth, which advocates that couples stick to having no more than two children. Knight takes things a bit further: 'I don't think the intentional creation of one more of us anywhere can be justified today. What we need to do is to phase out human beings from the biosphere because one species, us, is wiping out the rest.'

Phasing out the human race by voluntarily ceasing to breed will allow Earth's biosphere to return to good health, he says. 'We're not just a bunch of misanthropes and anti-social, Malthusian misfits, taking morbid delight whenever disaster strikes humans. Nothing could be farther from the truth. Voluntary human extinction is the humanitarian alternative to human disasters,' says the movement's website.[3]

Actually, the website is more witty than gloomy, using banned condom ads, comic strips and video animations to get its message across. 'I chose not to contribute to the problem,' says cartoonist and video-maker Nina Paley, who opted for sterilization. 'In terms of real impact on the planet the best thing you can do is not have a child.'

Researchers from Oregon State University have calculated that the carbon legacy of one child over a lifetime is 9,000 metric tonnes, the equivalent of a year's worth of emissions from 1,700 cars. For a nation in love with the car, that figure has pulling power.

Refreshingly, VHEMT does not identify 'the problem' as Africans or Asians with high fertility rates but applies its logic to all of us – and especially to the US which, while having only five per cent of the world's population, manages to consume a quarter of the world's energy resources. The movement also deftly unpicks the layers of conditioning that pressure people to procreate, pointing out that you can like children and engage with them without being their parents.

In many cultures heterosexual marriage and procreation are obligatory. Other possibilities are socially censured. Non-procreative same-sex relationships are not just frowned upon but illegal in more than 70 countries. In some they are punishable by death. In patriarchal societies especially, fertility is prized and having many children proves prowess and status.

The pressure to breed is exerted in liberal societies too, albeit in more subtle ways. Parents of adult children will openly 'look forward' to having grandchildren and will be disappointed if they are 'denied' the opportunity by their 'selfish' children.

For green activists considering parenthood the issue is especially thorny, as this contributor to *Earth First Journal* indicates: 'Does the decision to bear a child contradict a life in defense of the wild? While those opposed to breeding may see the act as selfish, those in activist communities who decide to have a child attempt to counter-balance a society of breeders who do not consider their environmental impacts.'

Not 'how many' but 'how'

Like so many population-control movements, VHEMT fixates on 'how many' at the expense of 'how'. The multiplier effect of population growth makes a difference, of course. But that does not make it 'the' problem. Again, the focus is shifted away from 'how' we engage with the natural environment, with each other, and with other species.

The possibility that we can change those relationships, that we are not necessarily chained in perpetuity to the disastrous fossil-fuel-driven engine of endless economic growth, endless consumption, endless destruction, seems to be ruled out. There is, in the VHEMT worldview, no alternative to 'business as usual'.

But we can choose to do things differently. Compared with the drama of ecocide and the loss of species, the stories of conservation success are modest. By upping policing and monitoring of deforestation in the Amazon, Brazil was able to report a 14 per cent drop in deforestation between 2009 and 2010, and its lowest level in 22 years, for example.[5] Around the world, there have been improvements in the way that forests are managed – for example, retaining corridors of 'forest' so that wildlife can move between conservation areas has helped to protect biodiversity.

The growing recognition of the land rights of indigenous peoples (typically better 'stewards' of Nature) has the potential for further protecting natural habitats. In December 2009 the UN General Assembly approved a resolution proposed by Evo Morales (and backed by the nine South American countries) to develop a Universal Declaration of the Rights of Mother Earth. The resolution calls on all countries to share their experiences and perspectives on how to create 'harmony with nature'. The consequences could be quite profound, especially in the legal arena. Currently activities that cause environmental damage – including climate change – are legal.[6]

At a grassroots level we have seen modest community projects grow into movements that are little short of revolutionary in their impact. Since 1977, when activist Wangari Maathai started the Green Belt Movement to combat deforestation in her native Kenya, over 44 million trees have been planted and thousands of women have trained in forestry, food processing, bee-keeping, and other trades that help them earn income while preserving their lands and resources. Communities around the world have been motivated and organized both to prevent further environmental destruction and to restore that which has been damaged. In Ecuador, the campaign to save Yasuní provides another positive model of how things could be done differently. The Yasuní Project involves getting richer countries to pay Ecuador to keep oil in the ground rather than exploit its reserves and, in so doing, destroy an extraordinarily rich and biodiverse area of tropical rainforest.

It should also be noted that many communities around the world already have low impact, low carbon ways of living.

We humans are capable of wrecking Nature – but we are also capable of protecting it, if we choose to. Even in the most unlikely places, in, for example, the dirty, hectic, core of civilization itself – the city.

Big bad cities?

The image is a common one. Population growth and its harmful effects are conveyed by the teeming, congested city scene. Satellite images provide further proof of the damage done: a sprawling grayish-brown cancer on our once-beautiful blue-green world.

As a species we are becoming increasingly urban, as more and more people abandon the countryside and flock to the cities. Already half of all humans live in urban settlements. By 2050 the UN predicts two-thirds of us will (see chart opposite).

This sounds like bad news for the planet. Cities create 80 per cent of greenhouse gases, we are told by

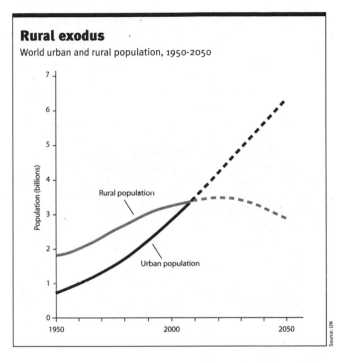

Rural exodus

World urban and rural population, 1950-2050

Rural population

Urban population

Population (billions)

1950   2000   2050

Source: UN

such bodies as the US-based Clinton Climate Initiative. But recently some experts have been questioning that figure – and coming up with some surprising results. These suggest that the trek to the cities might even be a good thing for the global environment.

David Satterthwaite of the leading sustainable development research organization IIED is one of those experts. When he re-examined the estimates of urban and rural carbon footprints he found that cities produce just 30 to 40 per cent of emissions – much less than previously thought. This was supported by similar research in the US.[7]

Further studies by David Dodman, also of the IIED, showed that the average Londoner produces half the emissions of the average Briton, while each New Yorker produces just 30 per cent of the emissions of the average US resident. In Brazil city dwellers emit even less, just 18 per cent of the average for their country.

It makes sense: it's easier and more efficient to provide electricity, sanitation and other services to people if they are living closely together. Transport is easier, too, and more likely to be public. The more densely populated a city is, the less people use private cars.

It is true that cities produce a lot of waste, but even this can be turned to advantage. The very scale of waste provides more viable opportunities for green initiatives – populous Seattle for example is siphoning off methane for use as fuel.[7]

The greening of cities is not just possible: it is already happening in many places, where people are enjoying the health and aesthetic benefits of city planning that incorporates more green areas and local initiatives such as city farms, organic vegetable growing and even 'guerrilla gardening'.

If cities are to realize their true green potential, however, it requires vision, planning and political will. People living in slums and polluted inner-city areas require access to decent services, such as electricity, sanitation, healthcare and education. But, here again, it is cheaper and easier to bring these to city shanty towns than to remote rural areas.

But what about China?

The rule that city-dwellers produce less greenhouse gas than their country cousins has one significant exception. In China, residents of Beijing and Shanghai now produce more CO_2 per head than people living in rural areas. But this does not mean that Chinese city dwellers are, as individuals, big polluters. What's pushing up the urban per capita figure is that many of the factories producing goods for Western consumption are located in China's big cities and those industries are major greenhouse gas emitters. If the emissions produced to make goods consumed outside China were taken into account, it would considerably increase per capita CO_2 in Europe, Australia, Japan and North America.

Changing Chinese lifestyles do have some part to play, however, as the tradition of recycling everything gives way to Western-style consumer culture. China is now the world's largest market for cars. It has also become a more throwaway society – symbolized by the millions of disposable chopsticks discarded each day. These chopsticks have pricked the public conscience, however. First environmentalists got active, proclaiming: 'Disposable chopsticks and destroying China's forests.' Greenpeace China launched a trendy campaign among urban youth called BYOC ('Bring Your Own Chopsticks') and 300 Beijing restaurants vowed to stop using disposable sticks. Then the government imposed 'luxury' taxes on throwaway chopsticks and set about banning other disposable items.[8]

Poisoned by some of the most polluted air in the world, China's city-dwellers breathe in a daily reminder of environmental limits. China both burns a lot of fossil fuel – and wastes a lot. Political economist Wenran Jiang calculated in 2005 that China was spending three times the world average on energy – and seven times what Japan spends – to produce $1 of gross domestic product. 'China needs to shift from a high energy-consumption model of development to a green model,' concluded Hu Angang, director of Tsinghua University's China studies center.[9]

Will it? There are some positive signs. Six gigantic windfarms are being built which will generate the equivalent of 100 coal-fired plants' worth of electricity. In 2009 China became the world's largest producer of wind turbines, overtaking Denmark, the US, Germany and Spain. In the same year it overshot its own 2010 target for producing wind by 150 per cent and it aims to quadruple this by 2020.[10]

China has also become the world's largest manufacturer of solar panels and is producing 30 per cent of global solar photovoltaics. Work is ongoing to develop low-cost modules to bring down the price of generating solar power. This could have a significant global impact. But, these developments need to be seen in the context of China's massive and ongoing exploitation of fossil fuels.

Much will depend on the strength and vitality of China's environmental and pro-democracy movements in the coming years. It will also depend on the country's ability and willingness to become a world leader in the energy revolution that has to come. China's own large population and desire for energy is a spur to innovation. The world can only pray it has the foresight not to emulate the West and wage war to secure oilfields. If that happens, voluntary human extinctionists will be left looking like optimists.

For many people, deciding not to have a child is appealing because, unlike global geopolitics, it is one of the few things that it is within their power to control. That's fine, but unless we all get a lot greener, deciding not to breed won't make anything like the necessary difference.

Human ingenuity can provide smarter, cleaner, greener ways of living. But the shift needs to happen at other levels too. In Bolivia they talk about *vivir bien* – 'living well'. Deriving from the indigenous Andean concept of *sumaq kawsay*, it is based on respect for Mother Earth or Pachamama.

These principles could provide the basis for an alternative development path that is not driven solely by ideas of growth, profit and capitalist accumulation. Bolivia's UN Ambassador Pablo Solón explains: 'We use terms like "living well" to describe a way of life that seeks not to live "better" and at the cost of others and nature, but in harmony with all.'[6]

Not only does this call for moderation, it also seeks to limit the rampant anthropocentrism that has dominated Western thinking and models of development for so long.

Is biodiversity different?

We can approach the challenge of increasing food or energy production by becoming less wasteful and more efficient. But biodiversity is not like that. It needs space. It needs large protected habitats.

US ecologist and demographer Fred Meyerson explains: 'Almost every conservation plan outside of zoos depends on safeguarding sufficient habitat to support viable populations and ecosystems over the long run, through the calamities of an erratic planet... Conservationists can sometimes overcome habitat loss and genetic bottlenecks and prevent extinctions by artificial techniques, such as captive breeding programs, invasive management and ecosystem manipulations, but such solutions are expensive, risky and temporary.'[11]

There's no avoiding it. To save the wild, habitats need to be conserved and we humans will have to find ways of using fewer of the Earth's resources per person. As our numbers rise over the next four decades, we are going to have to consume ever more wisely and carefully. City living might help. Renewable energy almost certainly will. But corporations will need to be kept in check and the notion that the wild is just there to be ransacked for human profit dismissed for good.

As mentioned at the start of this chapter, the world is going through what the experts call its sixth mass extinction. Sad as it is to lose species, some will become extinct and others will appear for the first time. In his provocatively titled book *Do we need pandas?*, Ken Thompson critiques sentimental mammal-fixated campaigns to save a particular species. But he is quite clear about the importance of safeguarding habitats and ecosystems.

For our own survival as well, we need to concentrate on ensuring that earth's ecosystems can support diversity – this includes fertility of land, size of forests and wetland, and soil pH.

That biodiversity – although we are apt to forget it – includes us too.

1 UPI.com, 21 Oct 2008. 2 AFP, 6 Oct 2008. 3 www.vhemt.org 4 www.planet-green.com 'No more children', 5 Sep 2009. 5 'Brazil: Amazon deforestation falls to new low,' news.mongobay.com 1 Dec 2010. 6 Vanessa Baird, 'To live...', *New Internationalist*, Mar 2010. 7 Shanta Barley, 'Escape to the City', *New Scientist*, 6 Nov 2010. 8 Karl Gerth, *As China goes so goes the world*, Hill and Wang, 2010. 9 Brian Bremner and John Carey, 'China's Wasteful Ways', *Bloomberg Businessweek*, 11 Apr 2005. 10 Wikipedia. 11 Fred Meyerson, 'Population, Bio-diversity and Human Well-being', Frontiers in Ecology and the Environment, 2009.

10 Conclusion

Some final words on the psychology of population watching, what we know, what we don't, and the inherent danger of all predictions...

A SURVEY CONDUCTED in the Netherlands asked people three questions. One: 'Are there too many people in the world?' Yes, replied the majority. Next: 'Are there too many people in the Netherlands?' Yes, again came the reply. Finally: 'Are there too many people in your community?' No, they replied.

The story is told by demographer Nico van Nimwegen and it illustrates a key point. 'Too many people' is almost inevitably too many *other* people. Not us.

History has shown us that if you scrape the surface of anxieties about population, you often find something else underneath. Be it related to race, class, religion, culture, politics or environment, the common fear is that of losing a portion of power or privilege.

Population is so often about something else, something other than sheer human numbers. And those numbers? What do they mean really? Projecting into the future, the sophisticated charts and figures create an illusion of solidity, of authority.

But even the most able experts, people who you might expect to know 'how many people can the earth support?', can't really answer that vital question because it depends on how those people live and how they share with each other.

Leading US demographer Joel Cohen wrote a book about it, thinking he would be able to provide a definitive answer. He found, he says, a range of 'political numbers intended to persuade people' but concluded the question was 'unanswerable in the present state of knowledge'.[1]

We don't, can't, know what the world will be like

in 2050. We know it will be different, but we don't know how. We can imagine, in a science fiction sort of a way, a clean, green, efficient post-carbon world or a burnt-out, flooded wasteland, teeming with hungry people and dying wildlife.

But if you try to envisage, in a more practical, realistic way, the world in 2050 with say nine billion people in it, what do you see? Is it basically our current world, with some minor adaptations, perhaps, to its technology, capacities, appetites and habits?

We humans have a habit of predicting doom for those who follow us after we are gone. The 20th century was peppered with experts who did not think humanity would make into the 21st. Which leaves me wondering just how much attitudes to population growth and the policies that flow from them have to do with what kind of person you are, whether you are more optimistically or pessimistically inclined.

If so, Jesse Ausubel is on the side of the optimists (or realists, depending on your proclivities).

He thinks we are already involved in 'resource sparing' mode with increasingly efficient use of land, energy, water and other materials that will allow 'humanity to grow in numbers, life-span or level of consumption while stopping the burden on nature becoming too disastrous.'[2] The fact that we still waste so much – see chapters 8 and 9 – is a sign of considerable future potential.

Ausubel also thinks that biology might lend a helping hand. Recent research, he says, suggests organisms do try to sense limits, using something called 'quorum sensing' to co-ordinate their reproduction according to local density of population and so avoid disastrous growth.

'You could say that fear-inducing articles... are social equivalents of quorum-sensing factors and we have responded to the signals,' he adds, citing higher farm yields and the development of more efficient turbines as examples of responses to such magazine or newspaper articles in the 1960s.

It's hard to believe, however, that there could by anything positive about the racist, sexist and classist agendas pushed by many under the guise of population concern.

In the end it all comes down to what we do, how we respond to the growing numbers over the next four decades, before population is projected to peak, decline and then stabilize. That is, of course, assuming the demographers are right and all those things happen. And if the planet is already feeling too crowded for you it's worth remembering that statistic about the world's current population fitting comfortably onto a land mass the size of Texas.

There are shortages that threaten the world and the survival of humans and other species within it – scarcities of equity, justice, genuine democracy and respect for nature. There is reason to feel panic when faced with global warming. The sluggishness of our political leaders and their supine relationship to corporate and elite financial power give further cause for alarm – and anger. But people having or not having babies is not the cause of these problems – and trying to control women's fertility seems a most unlikely solution.

Having said that, population is a devilishly slippery topic. Sometimes the only thing that seemed certain to me as I was writing this book was the caveat frequently expressed by demographers themselves – that population is as complex and ultimately unpredictable as human nature itself.

I am reminded of an experience I had in Mozambique in 1988, a time of civil war and hunger. I was interviewing a local reproductive health promoter and remarked that her job of convincing people of the benefits of family planning might not be so hard in such dire times. 'On the contrary,' she replied. 'The

Conclusion

birth rate is going up. You have to understand, there is so much misery around, children are our only joy. A new child brings a feeling of hope.'

There are some things that can be said with a degree of certainty. History has shown us time and again that target-driven population policies create a rationale for some of the most cruel and intrusive human rights violations. Furthermore, in many countries where the birth rate was forced down – as in China – the decline was already occurring before the policy was introduced. Countries without targets but where women have been empowered by better access to education and contraception – as in Brazil – have also achieved dramatic reductions in the birth rate, but without cruelty.

When women can make their own fertility choices, without pressure, without coercion, it is better for them, better for their families, better for their communities and better for the world, too.

One reader, a man as it turned out, took it a step further in a letter he wrote to me on the subject. To those concerned about population growth, he said, there is a simple solution: let women run the world.

1 Robert Kunzig, 'Population 7 billion', *National Geographic*, Jan 2011 2 Jesse Ausubel interviewed by Alison George, 'Ingenuity wins every time', *New Scientist*, 26 Sep 2009.

Resources

Organizations

United Nations Population Division (UNPD), New York
www.unpopulation.org

United Nations Population Fund (UNFPA), New York www.unfpa.org

Population Reference Bureau (PRB), Washington DC www.prb.org

International Union for the Scientific Study of Population (IUSSP), Paris
www.iussp.org

International Planned Parenthood Federation (IPPF), London www.ippf.org

The Guttmacher Institute, New York http://guttmacher.org

International Institute for Environment and Development (IIED), London
www.iied.org

The Corner House www.thecornerhouse.org.uk

Population Reference Bureau, Washington, DC, factsheets and online
discussions www.prb.org

International Institute for Applied Systems Analysis (IIASA) www.iiasa.ac.at

Worldwatch Institute www.worldwatch.org

Books

Fatal Misconception, Matthew Connelly, Belknap Harvard, 2008

Reproductive Rights and Wrongs, Betsy Hartmann, Southend Press, 1995

Peoplequake, Fred Pearce, Eden Project Books, 2010

More, Robert Engelman, Island Press, 2008

Population and Development, Frank Furedi, Polity Press, 1997

Journals/periodicals

Different Takes, The Population and Development Program at Hampshire
College,

Amherst, MA 01002-3359 http://popdev.hampshire.edu/

New Scientist, London, www.newscientist.com

The Corner House, 'Re-Imagining the Population Debate', Larry Lohmann,
The Corner House, 2003 www.thecornerhouse.org.uk

Index

Index